Working with Parents
of Young Children
with Disabilities

Early Childhood Intervention Series

Series Editor
M. Jeanne Wilcox, Ph.D.

Working with Parents of Young Children with Disabilities by Elizabeth J. Webster, Ph.D., and Louise M. Ward, M.A.

Pediatric Swallowing and Feeding: Assessment and Management edited by Joan C. Arvedson, Ph.D., and Linda Brodsky, M.D.

Working with Parents of Young Children with Disabilities

Elizabeth J. Webster, PH.D.
PROFESSOR EMERITUS,
MEMPHIS STATE UNIVERSITY

Louise M. Ward, M.A.
PROFESSOR EMERITUS,
MEMPHIS STATE UNIVERSITY

SINGULAR PUBLISHING GROUP, INC.
SAN DIEGO, CALIFORNIA

Singular Publishing Group, Inc.
4284 41st Street
San Diego, California 92105-1197

Typeset in 11/14 Bookman by So Cal Graphics
Printed in the United States of America by BookCrafters

Library of Congress Cataloging-in-Publication Data

Webster, Elizabeth J.
    Working with parents of young children with disabilities /
Elizabeth J. Webster, Louise M. Ward.
        p.   cm. — (Early childhood intervention series)
    Includes bibliographical references and index.
    ISBN 1–879105–46–2
    1. Parents of handicapped children.   2. Handicapped children
—Rehabilitation.   I. Ward, Louise M.   II. Title.   III. Series.
    [DNLM: 1. Child Development Disorders.   2. Handicapped.
3. Parent—psychology.   WS 105.5.H2 W378w]
RJ138.W44   1992
362.4'083—dc20
DNLM/DLC
for library of Congress   92-49909
                                                                      CIP

CONTENTS

For the many parents and
students who have shared
their thoughts and questions
with us and from whom we
have learned so much.

FOREWORD

When recent changes in social policy regarding at-risk infants and young children are considered in conjunction with advances in theoretical conceptualizations and associated research, it is clear that early childhood intervention is emerging as a unique and dynamic area of scientific inquiry across multiple disciplines. The *Early Childhood Intervention Series* provides state-of-the-art information about interventions focusing on families and their infants and young children who are at-risk for or have diagnosed disabilities. As readers will readily recognize, this is no small task. The "art" of effective intervention practices is continually subject to refinement and improvement of existing practices as well as introduction of entirely new ideas and approaches. As is the case with most topics subject to a rapid surge in scholarly attention, new findings and ideas are often steps ahead of their practical application, creating what many regard as a research-to-practice gap. Books in this series have been designed and prepared with an eye toward reducing this gap and assisting early childhood intervention personnel in becoming consumers of current theoretical and empirical information. The topics in the series are wide ranging and through explicit examples and discussion in each of the individual books offer a wealth of practical information to assist us all in providing the most effective interventions for families and their infants and young children.

As the first book in the series, *Working with Parents of Young Children with Disabilities* provides essential information for personnel across all disciplines involved in provision of services to infants and young children. This is a book that should be read and periodically re-read by all professionals who do, or will, interact with families of young children with disabilities. The concept of family centered services has emerged as a philosophy and mandate for the design and provision of early intervention services. Families of infants and young children with disabilities clearly have unique strengths and needs that must be understood and addressed in the process of formulating workable family–professional collaborations. Accordingly, early intervention personnel must have the skills and knowledge that will enable them to discover and learn about family strengths and needs. While some personnel may equate the concept of family centered services with the individual family service plan (IFSP), a truly family centered model has its beginnings well before the creation of an IFSP and continues well after such a document is in place. At the roots of this ongoing relationship with families is effective communication, a process exemplified in *Working with Parents of Young Children with Disabilities*. As readers will soon see, effective communication is a dynamic and at times taxing process that requires high levels of professional skill.

Webster and Ward provide us with the benefit of their substantial expertise, careful analyses, and sensitivity through their discussions of real families and real issues regarding their young children. I feel certain that readers will share in my recognition of many issues in the book. I feel equally certain that readers will share in my feeling that this book functions as a guideline for establishing and maintaining effective collaborations with families.

M. Jeanne Wilcox
Series Editor

PREFACE

It is now clearly understood that all those who treat a young child with a disability must necessarily work closely with that child's parent(s) and family members to plan and maintain effective treatment (see, for example, Roberts, Wasik, Casto, Ramey, 1991). Although the professional usually has a great deal of information about the child's diagnosis and condition, often very little is known about the parent(s) and the home situation before the first meeting of parent and professional. (Please note that here we understand parent to mean the child's primary caregiver.)

Professionals' lack of knowledge about the thoughts, feelings, and behaviors of the parents they will see is unfortunate because parents will bring to the initial meeting with professionals many unresolved issues and both positive and negative emotions, ideas, and attitudes. These forces will inevitably influence all collaboration.

We will highlight some of the major issues typically experienced by parents of children with disabilities and some of the emotions they engender. Of course, emotions, attitudes, and ideas are fluid, changing, forces, often changing very quickly. A parent's current state will be reflected in his or her behaviors in each interaction with those who treat his or her child. When the professional has some understanding of the parent's life situation and current emotional and attitudinal sets, certain parental behaviors will not be as frustrating. Rather, they can be seen as behaviors that must be coped with so that parent and professional can collaborate productively.

Each parent is unique; not all of them will struggle with all the issues and emotions discussed here. Most parents of children with disabilities will, however, cope with some of these issues because these concerns and emotions *are* typical.

Our intent is to expand professionals' understanding of these parents, not only to increase their effectiveness but also to help them feel satisfaction in this aspect of their work. If this book enriches and expands workers' vital contacts with parents of young children with disabilities, it will have fulfilled its purpose.

The format of the book has been chosen to keep its content clearly rooted in the reality of parents' life situations. The issues presented here have been discussed with us in various individual and group counseling sessions and in parent workshops. Each chapter highlights one or two such issues by reporting anecdotes from these sessions, sometimes in a parent's own words, sometimes paraphrased. Parents' names have been changed, their stories have not.

Each chapter also contains our commentary. The comments are designed to help professionals recognize the implications of these issues not only for parents but for the professionals who work with them. The intent is to help professionals cope with such issues as they arise. Chapters also contain suggestions for additional reading. These references are intended primarily for professionals, but some may be appropriate for parents, too. Giving parents reading material is no substitute for face-to-face discussion with them, but many parents like to read for additional information and help.

We appreciate all the support we received as we prepared this book. We are especially grateful to our editor and friend, Jeanne Wilcox, for her creative and helpful ideas and suggestions, and to Betty Farber, Arthur Farber, and Christopher Clement for the various ways they assisted in our learning to use the word processor.

INTRODUCTION

Professionals need to understand as much as possible about parents of young children with disabilities so that they can better carry out four major functions that professionals serve. These functions are so interrelated that all may be served in any given encounter, but we will separate them here for discussion.

1. *To give information to the parent.* Each specialist has information parents need. Thus professionals must understand each parent in order to judge the amount and kind of information that individual can absorb at one time and to know how to put the information into language the parent will understand.

2. *To obtain parents' information.* Each parent has a wealth of constantly updated information obtained from watching the child's behavior and knows the most about the family context in which the child lives. This ongoing information is available nowhere else because parent, child, and family situations are subject to frequent and sometimes drastic changes, which make case histories quickly outdated. Professionals need the up-to-date information parents can provide, and therefore must develop the skills to listen carefully to parents' input.

3. *To help parents understand and clarify their own ideas, attitudes, emotions, and behaviors.* Almost all parents need help in sorting out their emotions and attitudes about their situations. They also need help with clarifying the information they are given about their children's disabilities, about treatment plans, and their roles in treatment. Professionals who listen

respectfully and with understanding to parents' quandries are the ones parents are likely to trust as helpers. Consequently, these professionals are the ones with whom parents will cooperate best.

4.   *To offer the parent alternatives for changing his or her behavior, or the behavior of others, and to assist the parent in making those changes.* This function incorporates all the others. The professional who can best help parents change is the one who understands which behaviors a parent agrees he or she needs and wants to change. In discussion with the parent, the professional will also understand which behaviors the parent thinks will be easiest and which hardest to change. Finally, this professional will quickly learn from working with a parent the amounts and types of assistance that parent will need in order to effect change.

In outlining these professional functions we have spoken of the need for professionals to listen to parents. It should be understood that we are referring to a particular type of listening behavior. This is the type of listening that Gordon (1975) called "active listening" and Webster (1977) termed "listening to understand," two terms for essentially the same process. It is the process used when one wishes to understand as much as possible about the ideas, emotions, and meanings that make up another person's world. It involves many ways of trying to "tune in" to what the other person is thinking and feeling at that moment. It includes not only listening to the person's words but also being sensitive to his or her voice, facial expressions, and other body language in an attempt to understand what all the cues may reveal about that person's ideas and emotions.

In the effort to try to glimpse the vast world of another person's meanings, the listener's first challenge is to delay making his or her own judgment; that is, the listener temporarily sets aside agreement or disagreement with what the other person says. The listener shifts into neutral, as it were. This neutrality enables the listener to focus his or her attention as completely as possible on the task of understanding the other's world of meaning, whatever it is. The final step in this kind of listening is to understand the other person's world well enough that this understanding can be communicated to his or her satisfaction.

This type of listening is often misconstrued as a passive process, when, in fact, it is one of the most demanding activities in which professionals engage, particularly in their interactions with parents. Although the professional must be comfortable with periods of silence, he or she cannot sit altogether silently, nor get by with nodding wisely and saying an occasional "uh huh." Neither can the professional talk more than the parent. Rather, the professional's most intense concentration is required in the effort to comprehend what he or she thinks the parent means and to say it in a conversational manner that conveys genuineness.

The active listening process requires the professional to make hypotheses or guesses about the parent's world. These hypotheses can be verbalized by asking a question (e.g., "Are you saying . . . ?s" or "How did you understand what was meant by that?"). Professionals' hypotheses also may be voiced as statements, some of them made so tentatively that they sound almost like questions (e.g., "I think you're probably feeling . . ." or "you must have felt pleased when you learned to do that!").

Professionals are taught to make evaluations, and to do so very quickly. There are times, however, when an alternative mode of response (active listening) is more appropriate and necessary. This in no way diminishes the importance of skill in making professional judgments, and more will be said about evaluation and judgment in later chapters. Here it is important to understand active listening as another skill that is crucial to professionals, although it may be difficult to learn to listen in this way. Active listening assists professionals in building parents' trust and thus in obtaining information otherwise unavailable. Active listening also helps parents to clarify their ideas, attitudes, and emotions so that they can really learn the new behaviors involved in collaborating fully in the treatment of their children.

Professionals who delay judgment and listen actively get to know parents as more than just people with problems. Although we will point out many problems and hard issues parents discuss, these troubles are not the whole of their experiences. Rather, they experience the whole gamut of emotions. They feel joy and satisfaction, hope and love; and they need to have these feelings understood, too. Many of the parents we have worked with have displayed a keen sense of humor, and our time with them has been punctuated by laughter as well as by tears. Professionals who think they will hear only about problems may subtly direct conversation according to this preconceived judgment. These professionals will miss the lighter dimension which is part of parents, and thus miss some of the enjoyment of working with them.

CHAPTER ONE

Parents' Earliest Reactions to Confirmation of Their Child's Disability

Professionals who first confront parents with the diagnoses of their childrens' disabilities will directly experience parents' initial reactions to the news. Professionals who talk with parents afterwards, as children's treatment proceeds, will hear retrospective accounts of parents' first emotional and behavioral responses to confirmation of their children's disabilities. It seems clear that even years later the emotions regarding the event are alive in many parents because they can describe in such detail how they felt and what they did.

From the many examples given by parents who have talked with us, we have chosen two cases that illustrate such reactions. In the first case the child was 18 months old when we first met her parents in a counseling group. In the second instance, the child had grown to adulthood when his mother talked with us.

Sharon, Doug, and Jill

Sharon's voice was husky and she seemed close to tears as she described her early reactions.

We knew before the baby was born she was a girl and we'd call her Jill. I was glad for a girl because we have one 4-year-old girl, and I thought I knew how to manage girls. But Jill came at 7 1/2 months and I was pretty groggy, but I heard the doctor say "Get this one to the Med (neonatal intensive care unit at another hospital). I really panicked! I knew she was dying and I started screaming. I guess you could hear me all over the OB unit.

About that time the obstetrician came in and told me to hush so he could explain. He said Jill's lungs weren't well developed and her heart was too weak to pump the fluid out of them and, because that also caused lack of oxygen, she probably had pretty severe brain damage. He said he didn't know whether she could make it, but then added, I thought cheerfully, "But you're all right and you'll be able to have other children!" I wanted to kill him! I was so angry! Furious with his lack of caring. Other children! I wanted *this* child and I wanted her *well*! I yelled at that doctor to get out, and he looked flabbergasted, but he got out. Doug looked ready to fight him, too, but he didn't say a word, just looked grim and held me while I sobbed. After that outburst, they kept me in the hospital an extra day, saying I was "emotionally unstable."

The doctor also advised Sharon not to see the baby for several days after she was discharged, advice she didn't take.

I hustled off to the neonatal unit the very next day, then wished I hadn't, although I don't think it would have helped to have waited. She looked dead, inhuman, bandaged here and there, tubes sticking out all over, hitched up to three machines, I thought I was going to vomit, then faint; but a nice nurse who must have seen a lot of first reactions led me gently out of there.

I spent most of every day for the next five months in that waiting room and met some women I've stayed friends with. We were all in the same boat, angry at God, at the doctors, at life. We'd cry together and ask, "Why me?" Every so often we'd be allowed to take peeks at our awful looking babies, and then we'd cry some more.

But sometimes we could laugh at ourselves or at funny things that our other children did and that helped. Also, the head pediatrician met with us once a week and he seemed understanding and answered as many of our questions as he could. That helped, too.

Every afternoon we'd try to help each other get in shape to go home and face our families. And everybody at home had the same old needs, and I was ragged! I don't think I'd have made it half sane if it hadn't been for that group of struggling women helping me, and then all of us trying to help the new ones who came in.

Sharon reported that it was two months before she held her baby, and described it as: "like holding a lump of grey clay." Many times she thought Jill was dead,

then she'd move or whimper. She still doesn't ever really cry, more like a whimper or moan you have to listen hard to hear. Each time I hold her now I feel some of that same panic I felt when I knew she was so badly injured, and I cry still, and ask, "Why?" "Why her?" "Why me?"

Doug also attended several of the parent meetings, usually saying little, but nodding often in agreement as Sharon talked. Then one night he said:

I want you people to know I was thoroughly devastated about Jill, too. Attorneys are supposed to be pretty logical about everything, but I couldn't find much logic in having my life turned upside down. Our baby was *so* hurt, and our older child cried for her mother and couldn't understand why the baby took so much time. My wife was a shambles and we snapped at each other a lot, I think partly because none of us slept through any night, and I felt powerless to really help. I wanted to cry right along with Sharon, but thought that wouldn't help either of us. Besides, "big boys don't cry."

Connie, George, and G.J.

Connie and George had two girls and fervently hoped their third child would be a boy, so both were delighted when George, Jr. was born. They called him G.J.

Connie said G.J. cried very little as a baby. At times he seemed flaccid and at other times "his whole body became completely rigid." When Connie became alarmed about this pattern, she took him to her pediatrician and described the behavior in careful detail. She said the doctor assured her that " 'You're needlessly alarmed; he's a normal healthy boy with a beautifully shaped head and body.'" Connie said, "G.J. *was* a pretty child, but that doctor didn't hear a word I said about what I thought were problems."

By the time G.J. was 3 months old, however, his parents knew there were major problems. Connie reported:

> He screamed when picked up or when there were relatively minor noises. In fact, there was no cuddling this baby. When someone attempted to hold him and look at his face, he became rigid, would flail his arms, and attempt to escape. If he tolerated being held at all, it was with his back to you so he could look away.
>
> He didn't attempt to turn over until he was almost 6 months old; he just lay still wherever we put him down. It was funny though, one day he began to sit up, then he learned to walk, although he never crawled, and as he could move around he

was fascinated by toys that moved and would play with them for hours. Once he got moving, though, he seemed to have good motor control. By the time he was about 9 months old he could work the TV remote control; he'd flip through all the channels and stare like he was fascinated by the pictures flashing by.

Each time Connie reported these behaviors to a pediatrician, and she saw several, the response was that G.J. was healthy but slow to develop. One pediatrician "lectured" her about worrying too much and explained to her that boys often are slower to develop than girls.

After a year of feeling that she was getting no help at all with "this strange child," Connie began to search frantically for a professional who would listen to her concerns, really examine G.J., give her a diagnosis of his problem, and offer some treatment. She took the boy to various diagnostic centers, usually taking him by herself because George was starting a new business that demanded long hours daily and often on weekends. She reported that as G.J. got older, he became increasingly hard for her to manage on these trips.

At each diagnostic interview Connie carefully described G.J.'s behavior. She told examiners about how he avoided people and often was heard laughing aloud when by himself, "like he was laughing at something in his own little world." She described his behavior of covering his ears at noises other people didn't find particularly loud. Connie also reported carefully what she had noticed about his motor skills.

At one diagnostic center, the diagnosis was "minimal cerebral dysfunction with emotional overlay." At another center, Connie said, "they acted like the skills I told them about were just my wishful thinking, because he was no doubt retarded, although a definite diagnosis couldn't be made this early." At a third center, she was told that those who tested G.J. were surprised that he did so well in some areas, such as fine motor skills and ability to match pictures, rather than showing depressed overall performance that most children with developmental disabilities did. However, these diagnosticians agreed G.J. probably was in the educable mentally retarded group and recommended he be enrolled in a preschool for children with such developmental disabilities.

Connie found such a class in her hometown, but in about three weeks the teacher told her she would have to withdraw G.J. because he was "so active and had mannerisms that disturbed the other children." Although terribly disappointed, she found a woman to tutor G.J., and this seemed a good arrangement. The tutor was impressed with G.J.'s ability to manipulate numbers far beyond what many children his age could do and was amazed by some of the thoughtful statements he made, albeit he spoke in a monotone. The tutor insisted he was not simply retarded, although she, too, had noted that he had developed such mannerisms as moving his fingers rapidly in front of his eyes, unexpectedly bursting into loud laughter, or holding his hands over his ears when there was a noise outside the room. The tutor urged Connie and George to keep seeking a proper diagnosis for G.J. in the hope of finding help for him with a group of children.

Finally, when G.J. was 8 years old and no one who had worked with him could reconcile his behavior with mental retardation, Connie and John took him to a clinic some distance from their home. There, after three days of testing, the staff psychologist told them the results of testing and discussed the findings. She said that all the professionals who had seen him agreed that G.J. had autism.

As the psychologist began to explain the implications of autism, Connie said George looked stricken, but he said only, "Well, now we know what's wrong," and immediately left the room. Connie said she thought George probably shed some tears in the hall where the psychologist could not see him. Connie said her own first response was:

> numbness. I just felt *flattened*! You know, like sometimes life nearly knocks you over, but you know you can get up again. This time I felt like I'd never get up. I was so busy trying to hold myself together, I didn't hear much else that the psychologist explained. I was just rational enough to know that George and I knew nothing about autism, and we needed to. So I asked the psychologist to send me the report and some references she thought would be helpful, so I could read them when I could concentrate better.
>
> I've thought about that time in the years since that awful day. I had known all along that something was terribly wrong with G.J., so I don't know why it hit me so hard to finally have someone put a name to it. I think I went into a *huge* depression. For a long, long time I couldn't sleep, and I cried almost all the time I was alone. It was one of the very few times in my life I didn't enjoy eating. And while I hated to be cross, I was *so* cross with everybody!
>
> One day I decided that if this was the way things were, I'd better get up and find some training for G.J. so I could feel like I was doing something besides sitting at home with him. That shifted my feelings a little, but I still felt so sad and still cried often, but never around George. I guess I thought he had his own problems and needed me to be strong, so we didn't talk about our feelings. In fact, I didn't

talk to anyone about how I felt, and I wonder now how it would have been if I had someone back then to talk to and let it all out instead of keeping it all bottled up. I was so tight I felt I could barely function with my family or anyone else.

Commentary

The emotions reported by these parents are representative of those many parents have discussed as their first reactions to confirmation of their child's disability. The themes have been essentially the same whether the disability was apparent at birth (as in the case of Jill) or diagnosed when the child was older (as with G.J.)

However, there is great variability in the extent to which parents express such emotions to the presenter of the diagnosis. For example, Sharon's response was dramatic and unmistakable; on the other hand, unless the psychologist talking to Connie about autism was sensitive to the many emotions stirred by the diagnosis, she probably saw a woman who appeared to accept the news quite coolly and calmly.

Although their ways of expressing it vary widely, confirmation of a child's disability creates a crisis situation for parents. All human beings experience crisis, and readers may be familiar with the quite predictable stages of reaction to it, perhaps designated by different names than we will use in briefly describing them here. Professionals need to be aware of stages of crisis reaction because the behaviors arising in each stage can have such dramatic effects on collaboration between parents and professionals.

Shock

Shock is the first reaction to a traumatic situation over which one has no control. The person may experience panic, combined with disbelief or denial that the event is happening. This first emotional reaction can be so overwhelming that it actually impairs the person's entire perceptual system. Thus the parent in shock may be unable to comprehend or remember information or instructions.

Ensuing anger also is typical; it stems from feelings of helplessness and powerlessness. This anger can be directed inwardly at oneself or outwardly at almost anyone else. In the case of parents of children with disabilities, common targets for anger are the physicians or other professionals who have confronted the parent with the diagnosis. Helpless rage can be directed toward God or toward life in general. In some cases spouses may take their anger out on each other.

It is important for professionals to understand that these shock reactions are *not* abnormal. They are typical reactions that have been discussed by many authors writing about parents of children with various types of disabilities (e.g., Buscaglia, 1975; Hickey, 1992; Lavin, 1989; Rollin, 1987; Shontz, 1965). Thus, at various times in their careers, all professionals will be confronted with parents in the stage of shock. It is crucial to subsequent parent-professional relations that at this time the parent be understood as someone who has been deeply hurt and feels powerless and out of control. This is not to say that at this stage all parents behave in a helpless fashion. Most often they can do what needs to be done for their children and cope relatively well with their other responsibilities at home or at work. But often they do their tasks in spite of great confusion and pain, and thus may appear to behave in rather mechanical fashion.

Realization

Following shock comes what we will call realization. Denial and disbelief give way to the parents' realization that their problems are real, continuing, and must be coped with. This realization is usually accompanied by great anxiety, which may be experienced intermittently or as an almost all pervasive emotion. Any reader who has experienced anxiety knows that it is an emotion that can be debilitating while one is gripped by it. Unlike fear, which usually has a specific target, in anxiety one often cannot say what one is anxious about. The target is obscure, often nameless, but almost paralyzing. As is the case with all emotions, the anxiety that comes when parents face their problems squarely will be reflected in their behavior: Sharon spoke of her tears and her continuing panic, Connie of her inability to sleep, her general "crossness," and her depression. These behaviors suggest continuing anxiety, and perhaps part of it is that in this stage parents begin to feel grief over the loss of the child they had hoped for.

Anxiety may diminish parents' functioning as collaborators in treatment for their children. For example, a parent may be unable to understand information and instructions without having them repeated, may be slow and awkward in learning how to work with the child, or may be so sensitive that he or she feels that the professional's suggestions are criticisms. In their anxiety, parents may display confusion or anger.

When confronted with a parent's anxiety-induced behaviors, a large part of the professional's job is to understand that the parent is anxious. Otherwise, the professional may think the parent is just being trouble-some, or stubborn, or is not quite bright. Professionals must apppreciate that at this time the anxious parent is just coming to grips with the need to provide for the child. Unfortunately, it is at this stage that many parents are labeled "emotionally unstable" or "difficult to work with." Some professionals seem to expect parents to behave strangely while in shock, but then expect the same people to somehow be transformed quickly into rational, well-functioning individuals. This simply is not the case with most parents. It also is unfortunate that once negative labels like "difficult" are attached to a parent, the labels tend to be passed on from one profes-sional to another, possibly creating a negative bias in those who later work with that parent.

Retreat

Most of the parents we have known, faced with the enormous tasks entailed in rearing a child with a disabil-ity, have said that they often feel overwhelmed and that they would like to retreat. One woman, having recounted all she had to do that day, chuckled and said, "Almost every day I wish I could run away and let someone else do it." The feeling of not being able to handle everything they need to can make parents feel very guilty, but most do not give up, and neither did the woman in the above example. Most parents do not behave in ways that are characteristic of the stage of retreat, such as seeming to be as confused as they were in the shock phase, seeming helpless, or abdicating responsibility for participating in their children's treatment (Simmons-Martin, 1976).

Parents who do go into retreat can be very trouble-some to professionals who are trying to get them actively involved in their childrens' programs. The practitioner who can understand why parents might get stuck in this stage also can understand that, with help, most parents can move beyond this stage.

We suggest that professionals routinely work in conjunction with parents to select the tasks parents are asked to do. Having parents' input into task selection is always important; it may be especially crucial for those who seem to be in the retreat stage. Parents can be asked to begin their work with their children by doing tasks that they say seem easiest *to them*. Parents can be asked to do only as much as they can at any one time. Professionals can find ways to reinforce each productive effort parents make. Such professional care for parents' worlds also can help to shorten the time spent in retreat.

Acknowledgment

The title for this final stage of reaction to crisis suggests that, although parents probably will always wish that their children did not have disabilities, there comes a time when they adapt to the facts of their situations and show their ability not only to rear their children, but also to assist in their treatment. Parents of children with disabilities will continue to feel some anxiety about their children. It also seems true that parents continue to mourn the loss of "the child who could have been," but they move beyond actively grieving so that they can do the best they can visualize doing for "the child who is." It is here that they become the most efficient and delightful people to work with.

Individual Differences in Reactions to Crisis

These constructs regarding crisis reaction are useful in understanding parents of children with disabilities, but we must strongly emphasize that not all parents experience all of the stages of crisis reaction. However, it can be assumed that the majority will grapple with most of them. It is also safe to assume that individual parents will move through the stages at varying rates. For example, one mother may be stuck in the shock phase for several months or even years; another may move in only a few days into the period of realizing that her child's disability cannot be denied, but must be dealt with. Some parents move almost immediately from realization to acknowledgment.

Parents also express their reactions differently. Some talk less about their anger and more about their fears. Others speak more of their guilt than of their bitter disappointment. Because of all this variability, it usually is impossible for the professional to pinpoint the exact stage of crisis reaction a parent is in. Nevertheless, an educated guess can be made if the professional listens carefully to what the parent says and watches carefully how he or she behaves.

Although it is tempting to think that parents need only to have information about the child's disability and assistance with his or her management, our experience and the literature suggest otherwise (Crutcher, 1991; Kushner, 1981; Rollin, 1987). Parents *must* receive more than information, particularly in the early period following confirmation of their children's disabilities. At this time they need to feel support, understanding, and compassion as they cope with their own emotions and behaviors.

The quality of future parent-professional relations may depend in large measure on the quality of help received early on. If parents are to have good working relationships with professionals, make use of professional information, and carry out the suggestions professionals give them, they must be in emotional shape to do so. Often the professional who first treats the child also is the first to help the parent become emotionally ready for collaboration.

Other Parents Can Be Helpful

Early in their attempts to cope with the crisis of learning that their children have disabilities, parents will have many questions, some that can be answered and some that will remain forever unanswerable. Professionals often find, as the pediatrician who worked with Sharon and the other mothers in our first example did, that parents can be seen in groups. Here all parents can be given information that pertains to all of them and have some of the questions they share answered.

Information giving is not the only advantage of putting parents together with other parents, however. Many parents have said, as Connie did, that early in their experience they had no one to talk with about their feelings of loss, anxiety, and guilt, and that they would have liked to share their feelings with others. Parents facing similar dilemmas, whether or not their children have the same disabilities, can offer each other support during this period of adjustment.

Professionals should note, however, that, although group support is helpful for many parents, some do not feel able to talk with other parents early in their experience of crisis, unless they are in a situation such as Sharon was. An example is a young woman whose husband and 3-year-old son were in an automobile accident in which her husband was killed; the boy survived, but with paraplegia. This woman sought counseling from the psychologist at the hospital where her son was receiving physical therapy. The psychologist suggested that she join a group of parents whose children also had disabilities. The woman refused, saying that she still couldn't face people who might talk about their family life. She said, "I cry so much, and I don't know whether I'm crying about my husband or my child or just my whole future. I guess I don't mind crying with just you, but I'd hate to have in front of a whole group." The counselor, of course, saw her individually.

After about three months of individual work, this woman said, "I think I'm ready to join your group now that I don't care so much whether I cry or not." She was enrolled in the group and did cry on occasion as she spoke of her husband's death or told of her son's struggles to get ready to learn to use crutches. She also added a great deal to the group. She listened to others carefully, spoke very compassionately to those who cried about their situations, and offered suggestions to those who asked for them. The point is that when parents are ready for interaction with other parents — and only they know when that is — groups of parents can be very helpful to each other.

Suggested Readings

Gordon, S. (1988). *When living hurts.* New York: Dell.
Kushner, H. S. (1981). *When bad things happen to good people* (Introduction and Chapter 1). New York: Avon.
Smith, P. M. (1984). *You are not alone: For parents when they learn their child has a handicap.* Washington, DC: National Information Center for Children and Youth.

CHAPTER TWO

Parents' Crises Continue

It would be more comfortable for both parents and professionals if, once parents had moved through the crisis of diagnosis, it were the last one they had to deal with, but that is not the case. Parenting a child with a disability means dealing over and over again with crisis situations that arise. With each new crisis, parents must live through at least some of the aforementioned stages of crisis reaction, and the professionals who are working with them at that time again see behaviors that accompany crisis. The following cases illustrate several common types of crises parents continue to encounter.

Denise, David, and Jim

Denise and David's active 4-year-old son, Jim, stuttered severely. The parents were very concerned about Jim's speech and its potential effect on his personality and relationships with other children. After much discussion, they agreed that Denise would take Jim for an evaluation for speech therapy, which she did.

During the initial interview with the speech-language pathologist, it was apparent that Denise and David had many conflicts about how to discipline Jim. Denise said that David thought she was extremely overprotective of the boy, and he thought this "coddling" contributed to his stuttering. She said that she did try to protect Jim because "David is so stern and harsh when he thinks Jim has done something wrong, and he forgets Jim is only 4." When the interviewer asked whether they argued about Jim in front of him, she admitted that they did. She said they always regretted later that they had argued about Jim when he was around.

Subsequently, Jim was enrolled in a preschool speech therapy program which included one hour a week in which the children's parents met with one of the clinic's parent counselors. When the counselor asked David to come with Denise to counseling, he said that because he was self-employed he thought he could come to most of the meetings, and did so.

In one of the early sessions with both Denise and David present, the counselor raised the topic of the conflict between parents about how to discipline their children. David said, angrily, "Well, *somebody* has got to discipline our boy or he's going to end up a sissy mama's boy!" Denise countered quickly, "But he's only 4 years old and you're too hard on him and too quick to punish!" After the counselor had listened with understanding to their outpouring of anger and then to their fears, she raised the possibility that they were feeding the behavior each disliked in the other; that is, as David became more strict, Denise became more overprotective, and vice versa. As their discussion continued, Denise and David considered this point and reluctantly agreed that each of them probably was making the other worse.

It took several additional meetings, and the help of the counselor and others in the group, before Denise and David could visualize some changes they thought they could make to effect more balanced, workable, and comfortable ways of relating with each other and with Jim. David said that he had thought a lot about the possibility that he had expected a great deal of his first son. He would agree to try not to be too stern if Denise would agree not to interrupt him to say how young and sweet Jim was. Denise agreed to that condition, even if it meant she had to go to another part of the house to avoid interfering. She agreed further to continue to work individually with the counselor on diminishing her fearfulness about Jim so that she would be less overprotective.

By the time Jim was discharged from therapy, Denise reported that she and David had tested a number of new ways of communicating with each other about the boy, even when they disagreed. She said they no longer argued in front of Jim, so that both of them felt less guilty about that. She reported further that David was enjoying playing with Jim in "4-year-old ways," and had taken the boy fishing on several occasions.

Sharon, Doug, and Jill

When Jill (the baby with multiple disabilities discussed in Chapter 1) was 6 months old, her mother was contacted by a teacher of the deaf. The teacher had received the hospital's list of babies who had been in their intensive care unit and were thought to have severe or profound hearing impairments. The teacher offered to provide a home pre-language training program for Sharon to help Jill respond to sounds, including speech, in the hope that later Jill could learn to use speech.

Sharon said:

Doug and I already knew Jill couldn't hear much and in some ways it was the least of her problems. I don't know why I did it, but I agreed to enroll her in that program. It turned out I really just set up more trauma for myself. It seemed the teacher who came to the house twice a week usually arrived when I was in the midst of some kind of crucial task, and just her being there was hard on me. When I got more realistic, I began to see very little point in the language training right then when there were so many other things I had to do that really made a difference in just keeping Jill alive. I was still feeding her formula through a tube in her side and constantly cleaning the tube. I had to give her oxygen several times a day and clean that tube, too, and learn to do the exercises the physical therapist showed me so Jill would have fewer contractions in her arms and legs. Each one of these jobs traumatized me every time I did them, and I was tense even when Doug helped me or did them himself; but they were absolutely necessary. I talked to Jill like she could hear me, but felt like she couldn't respond much yet. So, after I had aired all my anxiety about the language training with the physical therapist, who also came twice a week, I decided the language work was a frill at that point. It also felt like one more thing I might make a mistake with.

I felt the trainer was disappointed in me, impatient, and annoyed that I wasn't enthusiastic about this work, so we dropped the program, and that *really* annoyed the trainer! I really felt put down by her! We're back in the program now that Jill can take formula by mouth and needs oxygen less often, but with a different trainer.

Commentary

Any professional, no matter what his or her speciality, who listens carefully to what parents say, and tries to understand what they mean by what they say, will hear about many types of continuing crises. For example, the speech pathologist who recommended speech therapy for Jim understood that Denise and David were in trouble with each other and recommended that both should come to the parent counseling sessions. It was the physical therapist who first heard Sharon say that language training with Jill added a crisis to her life and listened as Sharon thought through ways to make her life less stressful. Often, the professional who listens to parents can provide help on the spot for these crises without referral to other professionals, although it must be recognized that sometimes referral is necessary.

Of the many types of continuing crises parents have reported, some seem to occur quite frequently. Some of the most common ones are discussed next.

Conflicts Within the Family

As Wyatt (1976), Crais (1991), and others have pointed out, professionals must treat children with disabilities and their parents as part of networks that include entire families. From this point of view, it is understandable that conflicts can occur not only between parents but also with other family members, such as grandparents, in-laws, and so on. Often these relatives disapprove of the way parents treat the child with the disability or are critical of the way other children in the family are treated. As one woman said angrily, "I have enough guilt already about my other children, I don't need my mother telling me how I neglect them!"

Other children in the family may resent the time their parents must give to the child with the disability. Some siblings express their resentment openly and quite vocally. For example, a mother whose 2-year-old was recovering from meningitis and required almost constant care at home, told of asking her 6-year-old daughter to bring something to her in the baby's room. The older child, who had already made several trips upstairs that morning, yelled, "Mom, just because she's sick and deaf, you're spending all your time with her and none with me! Aren't you *ever* going to play with me again?" On the other hand, siblings may be silently sullen, behavior the parent understands to reflect children's anger or resentment.

Intergenerational conflicts occur in many families, whether or not one of their members is a child with a disability. It also is possible that parents of children with disabilities may react more strongly to the judgments and criticisms of other family members because of the many other stresses they carry. As one woman said, "I was super sensitive; no one could look at me hard or I'd think I was being criticized."

Another source of family conflict can occur when the father of a child with a disability is in the home and is overlooked by professionals treating the child. Professionals most often work closely with mothers or other female caregivers in treating children because this work is usually done during the day when fathers are working. Professionals who are sensitive to the needs of fathers, and sensitive to the conflicts that can occur between spouses of children with disabilities, will find ways to reach out to fathers. For example, the professional who saw Denise and David (in the example earlier in this chapter) called David to say he was a very important helper for his son, and to invite him to come to the discussion group that was part of Jim's treatment. In this case, the father could arrange his schedule to participate. Many fathers do not have this flexibility, and the professional must be flexible if he or she is to meet with a father. Some options include meeting for lunch, meeting after the father's work day ends, or conducting evening meetings. If face-to-face meetings are not possible, the professional can call the father to discuss questions he might have, or send him a note inviting him to call the professional. Professionals whose focus is on family oriented treatment will endeavor to make adjustments so that fathers, too, can feel involved and supported, and don't have to rely just on their wives to transmit professional information.

The professional who hears about family conflicts of course cannot change the behavior patterns of all members of that family. However, it is true that when the behavior of one family member changes, the whole configuration changes. Thus, the professional can listen to understand the problems as the parent sees them. Often the professional can suggest alternatives in the ways the parent could respond to the family members who are troubling to him or her. The professional also can support the parent's efforts to test new behaviors in relation to family members.

In the case of siblings, professionals can help parents learn to talk directly with their children about needs and feelings the children experience. These feelings can include fear and guilt. As Brazelton (1989) has noted, children have fears of many kinds, particularly about things they don't understand. Many children don't understand their brothers' or sisters' disabilities and, therefore, may fear that they will do something wrong in relation to their brothers or sisters. Many children also experience guilt when something goes wrong in a family, feeling they may have caused it. In short, children can feel the same universe of emotions that their parents experience, and parents can be helped to understand their children's feelings.

Children often can be helped to work though their negative feelings if given the chance to talk about them with understanding parents. Faber and Mazlish (1980) have suggested that parents try not to make up their minds about what their children think and feel. If parents can delay judgment, they can listen compassionately to what their children say. Parents can then let children know that it is all right to have such emotions. Parents may need to place strict limits on the behaviors that stem from their children's emotions, but they cannot, and should not, try to limit these emotions.

The suggestions given by Faber and Mazlish to parents for entering into dialogues with children are very much like the suggestions we made to professionals in the introduction to this book. These suggestions may be very hard for parents to follow when they themselves are experiencing great emotional upheaval. However, when parents are able to listen openly and with understanding to their children, the children will no doubt feel better. The children of parents who actively listen to them also may be less of a worry to their parents.

Provision for Other Children

In addition to trying to provide for the emotional needs of other children in the family, parents must arrange for them to be cared for during the times the child with a disability must be taken to various places for treatment. One mother said:

> It was hell to try to keep my daughter entertained in safe ways while I took Joe [who had cerebral palsy and needed several therapies] for his appointments. It was awfully expensive for baby sitters, too. I was really grateful when she got old enough to go to school; now I only have to worry in the summer. Isn't it a sorry shame when you want your kid to hurry and grow up to make your life easier?

Most parents we have known have admitted they made many mistakes in rearing their children, and some have said they felt a great deal of guilt about how they handled certain situations. But *all* of the mothers we have talked with who had children with disabilities have expressed guilt that other children in the family paid a high price for the care required by the child with the disability. They have said they thought their other children missed out on attention, even though the siblings loved and helped to care for the child with the disability. Professionals should expect to hear this theme again and again.

Reactions of Those Outside the Family

Parents of children with disabilities also are very sensitive to the reactions of neighbors, friends, and strangers to their children. Two examples illustrate this point.

Mary, a 62-year-old grandmother, was rearing her granddaughter, Sara, a friendly, outgoing 4-year-old with Down syndrome. Sara was likely to run up to strangers, hug them, and attempt to talk to them, although her speech was unintelligible. Mary told a parents' group that she couldn't afford baby sitters, so she had to take Sara with her wherever she went. She said, "I'm almost physically sick the morning before I have to take her to the grocery store. I know people are going to stare at her, maybe ask why she can't talk. And God forbid if she hugs them, they back off *so* fast and look horrified."

The other parents nodded their understanding. Frank, who owned a business in which his trucks took lunch and snack items to construction sites and was rearing his 2-year-old son with cerebral palsy by himself, nodded in understanding,

> I know what you mean. When I get an emergency call, there's no time to get someone to keep Taylor and I have to take him with me. He gets all kinds of looks from the men I take stuff to, and it makes me mad. Taylor smiles a lot, and I understand it's just a reflex, but one day a guy I know well actually said to me, "What's your crippled little kid got to smile about? I'd put him away." I rushed the guy, but other men pulled me back, probably a good thing. He was bigger than I am and getting beat up wouldn't have helped my feelings at all.

Many parents resent others' reactions to their children with disabilities and feel powerless to handle these situations. The professional who listens can understand this resentment, point out the fact that others' reactions and remarks cannot be controlled, and assist parents in finding ways to control their own reactions.

Working with Different Professionals

Our work in professional training programs, where there were changes in the graduate students who provided much of the direct treatment for children, led us to realize that such changes can create a crisis situation for many parents. Sometimes, indeed, the children adjusted more easily to the change of personnel than did their parents. This potential source of parents' stress should be kept in mind. Personnel changes are not uncommon in any professional setting, and as the child with a disability gets older, new professionals (e.g., teachers) will enter the life of the child and his or her parents. Parents are then confronted with, and must adjust to, different personalities working with them and their children. When a parent has difficulty adjusting to a new person, it often tells more about the parent's insecurity with the unknown than about the new professional.

Most professionals can easily understand a parent's fear of the unknown and of change and can create an environment that helps the parent overcome such fears. These professionals also realize that parents' problems in learning to relate to a new person will be particularly acute if the new person holds a different point of view—however slight the difference may be—from one with which the parent has become comfortable. If the new professional's different viewpoint is part of the problem, the professional's responsibility includes carefully explaining his or her ideas and what he or she hopes to accomplish. The professional also needs to confirm that the parent understands the professional's message as it was intended. Just asking, "Do you understand?" or "Do you have any questions?" doesn't encourage dialogue. Many people don't want to admit they don't understand, nor do they want to ask a question lest it appear to be an unimportant one. The professional who uses sentences such as, "Tell me how you react to what I've said," "Tell me how you understand this point," or "I'd like to hear how this information is useful to you" encourages parents to think about ideas. Statements like these also encourage parents to respond at greater length rather than with just "yes" or "no."

A Crisis is a Crisis for the Person Experiencing It

The types of continuing crises we have discussed have been the most common ones in our experience. This is not to say that parents do not experience many crises not listed here or that individual parents will react to the crises we have discussed with the same degree of intensity.

Many of the situations that a parent describes as crises will seem truly critical to the professional; others will seem fairly mundane. It is usually quite easy to want to help alleviate situations that seem critical to the listener, but it is easy to overlook items that seem critical to the parent when they seem less important from the professional's point of view. Professionals must remember that they do not live in the parent's world and, therefore, *cannot* judge whether or not a particular event is crisis producing. It is much safer to assume that, if the parent says something creates a crisis, it does *for that person at that particular time.*

Often professionals can help a great deal in alleviating parents' crises while doing activities that are part of their regular duties. For example, when a physical therapist and parent are engaged in helping a child with his or her exercises, the therapist can listen to the parent's discussion of a crisis situation and respond in ways that help the parent clarify his or her emotions. This was the case in the earlier example when the physical therapist helped Sharon sort out her feelings about enrolling her daughter, Jill, in language training. Following this clarification, Sharon was able to decide what she wanted to do about the situation. It is also possible that a specialist, in the course of other duties, can give information or make suggestions to help a parent deal productively with a crisis .

Professionals Can Induce Crises

Sometimes, even in their best efforts to help children and parents, professionals unintentionally create a crisis for parents. One of the authors vividly recalls a situation that arose when she was directing the cerebral palsy division of an outpatient clinic. The children came to the clinic five mornings per week, and a group was held for an hour one day a week for parents of children in the program. Vera enrolled her son, John, who had severe spasticity, in the program when he was 2 years old.

When John started his training he could not turn over or crawl when put on his stomach. John's attendance in the program was almost perfect, and Vera said she "counted on" meeting with the other parents so she was there regularly. John, a bright-eyed, often smiling child, was in the program for three years. During this time he learned to crawl, to sit alone, then to pull himself to a standing position. He could not walk without assistance, but his hand coordination had improved to the point that he could stack large blocks and put large pegs into the proper holes on a pegboard. He could also point slowly but accurately to very small pictures of objects when asked to do so.

Although John seemed to quickly comprehend language as complex as three-part instructions and he understood stories, as indicated by his pointing to the correct pictures when asked about the stories, he could not speak. He communicated only by nodding or pointing and making noises. He moved his mouth as if trying to talk, and then seemed very distressed when no words came. Vera also was distressed when she couldn't understand what John meant as he tried to communicate with her.

In light of John's progress, and because the clinic director felt her program did not have the equipment needed to assist John further with communication, she wanted to refer John to a learning center. The director explained her reasons for the referral to Vera, also explaining that the learning center was a residential program from which John would go home every weekend. The director thought Vera would welcome the news, but instead she burst into tears, saying, "You can't send him away; this is home to him, and the only place I can talk about my problems!" The director attempted to explain again, but then realized her job was to listen to the mother. What she heard was a woman in crisis, who felt abandoned, robbed of a place where she felt comfortable and a place that her child enjoyed.

Vera went through a period of anger at all the personnel in the program, and then said she was going to refuse to follow the referral. The director assured her that the choice was hers and that, even if John was not in the program, she could continue with the parents' group. However, the director emphasized that the clinic's program had done all it could for John's communication skills. Therefore the clinic could not ethically continue to enroll John and to take her money when it could not give John the service he now needed.

After a series of conferences with the director in which Vera aired her fears and her disappointment, she did enroll John in the learning center. She continued to attend meetings with parents whose children were still in the clinic's program and later told the parent group that, "Your kids are learning to talk and I don't know if John ever will, but he has a machine that he's learning to use. It prints the word when he points to its picture, and what a relief it is to know more about what he means."

Other ways professionals can create crises for parents stem in part from the dictates of their work. For example, many professionals must make home visits because children are unable to come to them. For some parents, the professional's regular visits to their homes constitute at least minor crises. As one woman with six children said,

> I like the physical therapy lady and the nurse; but on the days they're coming, I feel like I'm having company. For company, you're supposed to have the house clean and kind of fixed up. My house is hardly ever really clean or fixed up. And hard as I try to keep the other kids quiet, they're always making some kind of noise. So to tell the truth I dread the visits of the nurse and the therapy lady. And to make it worse, they come on different days.

Professionals whose work entails going into parents' homes can be aware that their visits may not be ideal from the parents' points of view. Although professionals cannot take away a parent's insecurity about home visits, they can be sensitive to how the parent feels and try to communicate a down-to-earth informality that can help put the parent more at ease. Certainly professionals should not try to take over and dominate the action during a home visit, for example, by giving directions to the other children who may be present. The homes into which professionals go to work are the parents', and parents rightfully are in charge.

Another situation that may induce a crisis for parents occurs when diagnostic testing must be done over several sessions. This situation often is unavoidable, but professionals must recognize that waiting for diagnostic results is usually very trying for parents. The longer the process takes, the more tension parents feel.

Some professionals feel they must be altogether silent until all their findings are in. They may think they are doing parents a favor by withholding all information and discussion until testing is completed. However, all professionals should recognize that the very act of taking their child for diagnosis is difficult for most parents. Most parents want to know at least whether the professionals are able to test their children, whether the children are cooperative, tired, and so forth. Parents also have a right to know something about the diagnostic process as it proceeds. The lack of some kind of supportive information along the way, prior to being bombarded with test results, sets up a crisis situation for many parents. As Connie (in Chapter 1) said of one of her experiences in taking G.J. for a battery of tests:

I was there for three days, and each day I expected them (the examiners) to say something about what testing they'd done that day or how things were going, but they'd only say, "We'll talk to you when all the tests are in." I was wild with worry when nobody would say anything. I didn't know whether they could really test him or not, and I had to wait a week to find out what they'd found.

Of course professionals should not give parents preliminary test results because parents may take them as final. Furthermore, later testing may make it necessary to modify early findings. Neither should professionals try to make everything seem all right when talking to parents when, in fact, things may not be all right. A case in point occurred when a psychologist was testing a young boy, Tim. Tim's mother, Kathy, was in a waiting room nearby and heard Tim crying for about the first 15 minutes of the first testing session, but when the psychologist brought Tim out, she told Kathy, "We had a wonderful time today!" Kathy, in reporting the incident, said dryly, "Makes you wonder what would give her a bad time." How much better it might have been for the professional to say something like, "It was pretty strange for Tim at first, but we got along well as we became acquainted," or "When Tim and I got over being strange to each other, we played with a lot of toys and Tim talked about them."

Given the limitations of neither revealing preliminary findings nor saying inane things designed to cheer parents, it is possible for the professional to tell parents that testing went well (when it did), to say that he or she is enjoying the child (when this is true), or to say (in cases such as Tim's) that things will be less strange to the child at the next session. Or the professional can simply state his or her understanding that waiting for more information can be hard for the parent.

Home visits and lengthy diagnostic sessions are among the situations that professionals cannot avoid. They can only do their best to make them as comfortable as possible for parents. A stressful situation for parents that *can* be avoided occurs when professionals fail to communicate with each other. When several professionals are working with the same child, which is most often the case, they *must* communicate with each other about what is happening. A parent cannot be expected to be the primary reporter to one professional on another professional's work with his or her child. Many parents experience it as a crisis when they have to act as the go-between for professionals, and this is understandable. Many also experience great anger at the noncommunicating professional, which also is understandable. An example may summarize this point.

A 3-year-old boy had a seizure one morning while at a learning center. The center's nurse called the boy's mother to say they had sent him to the emergency room at the hospital the family had listed as the one where their pediatrician worked. The mother asked the nurse to call the pediatrician and explain what had happened. The nurse said she would, but when she had not called by late afternoon, she received a phone call from the very irate pediatrician. The mother was also angry, saying, "I wasn't there, so how could I know how my boy looked and what happened? Besides, even if I had been there, I don't know all that medical jargon they can talk to each other with."

There are many other examples of professionals who fail to communicate with each other: a neurologist who delays sending his or her report to a child's pediatrician, a speech-language pathologist who does not communicate with a child's preschool teacher, a pediatrician who refers a child to a neurologist but fails to communicate the precise reason for the referral, and others. Professionals must communicate not only with parents but with each other about the children they treat if total treatment plans are to be effective. Perhaps professionals would do better in this area if they thought of their communication as helping to prevent potential crises, not only for parents but for themselves and other professionals as well.

Professionals' use of the "jargon" of their specialities can have a bearing on parents' experience of crisis. For example, on the advice of a pediatrician, a young man took his 3-year-old son who was blind to be enrolled in a residential school for the blind. The father reported:

> I was so scared, nervous about Bill anyhow, and when I drove up to the building, I was glad Bill couldn't see it. It looked like a prison. But I carried him in and a nice lady met us and another nice lady took Bill, so the first one could explain to me what they'd do for him. Bill cried when he left and I nearly cried, too, it was so awful seeing him go. The first lady started explaining, and I got the idea about Bill's schedule okay, and that he could come home on weekends. But when she started talking about "optic nerves" and "tactile sense" and "compensation," she started losing me. To me, "compensation" was pay, and I didn't know "tactile" at all. The lady asked if I had any questions, and I had a lot; but I asked just a few questions, not very good ones, I guess, because I felt so *dumb* by that time. They brought Bill back in so I could say I was going and I'd be back for him Friday, and he cried some more and I got out of there because I was crying, too, and feeling very, very dumb.

There are several messages here for professionals:

1. Sometimes, even though we don't intend to create problems, the nature of our work can cause crises for parents.

2. Certain professional behaviors can be thoughtless of parents' situations.

3. Professionals must be aware of their power to add to parents' experiences of crisis, and must do all they can to be considerate of parents' worlds and thus guard against thoughtlessly creating crises for them.

Suggested Readings

Crais, E. (1991). Moving from "parent involvement" to family-centered services. *American Journal of Speech-Language Pathology, 1*(1), 5–8.

Crutcher, D. (1991). Family support in the home: Home visiting and public law 99–457, a parent's perspective. *American Psychologist, 46*(2), 138–140.

Faber, A., & Mazlish, E. (1980). *How to talk so kids will listen and listen so kids will talk*. New York: Avon.

Lang, D. (1990). *Family harmony: Coping with your "challenging" relatives*. New York: Prentice-Hall.

CHAPTER THREE

The Search for a Cure

When we discuss parents who search for a cure for their children's disabilities, we do not mean parents who carefully select from possible treatment plans or sites of treatment. It is appropriate and desirable, of course, for parents to choose the treatment that best suits their child, their family, and their current life situation. Often, indeed, a professional will suggest to parents that they find a service that is closer to home, uses different equipment, or is in some way better suited to their needs than what the professional can offer.

However, some parents engage in a desperate effort to find someone or something that will alleviate their problems, or at least improve their situations, and become what professionals sometimes call "shoppers." Such searching may be part of the stage of retreat, or it may be a result of denial because it often happens early in the period after confirmation of a child's disability. Most professionals have known some parents who were shoppers, and have been frustrated by their behavior. The following are examples of parents who searched frantically for ways to quickly alleviate their pain.

Frances and Katy

Frances was divorced when her only daughter, Katy, was less than a year old. Frances was concerned that Katy's development seemed different from that of the other children she observed, and at first she thought the differences could be attributed to the divorce. However, her family and friends also noticed that Katy was slow to develop. They convinced Frances that all of Katy's problems might not be emotional, and they urged her to find out what was the matter by having Katy thoroughly examined. Frances was reluctant to think there was anything wrong with Katy that time and her loving care couldn't take care of, although she, too, was suffering from the strain of her divorce. Finally, at the urging of other family members, Frances agreed to have Katy tested, and when the child was about 2 years old Frances took her for evaluation at the medical center in the city in which they lived.

Physical examinations revealed that Katy was in good health but that she displayed an abnormal EEG pattern. During behavioral testing, her play included walking abruptly and rapidly away from one toy to find another. She had difficulty with age-appropriate fine motor tasks. At no time did she sustain eye contact with the examiners, nor did she speak to them, although she uttered several unintelligible words while looking at various toys.

The diagnosis was made of cerebral dysfunction resulting in lack of fine motor coordination and severe apraxia. A social worker explained the findings to Frances in understandable terms. She readily agreed with the diagnosis, having said earlier that her chief concern was that "all Katy's movements are very jerky and uncoordinated, and though she seems to want to talk, when she moves her mouth, the words just won't come out."

A treatment plan was then outlined. The plan included physical therapy and play activities designed to elicit some eye contact with the speech-language pathologist and some simple single word utterances. When Frances first heard the plan, she nodded in what seemed to be understanding and agreement. Then she asked how soon Katy would be able to talk, and when the professional declined to speculate, Frances said she'd have to think about the recommendation. She said she would call when she had decided what to do.

Those who had diagnosed Katy and planned her therapy heard nothing from Frances for two years. When she did return, the program director who talked with her thought she seemed very subdued and discouraged. She explained that she had taken Katy to four "big name" medical centers, hoping that "perhaps they'd know of some kind of surgery or other treatment that would help Katy more quickly." Nowhere had she found such a "quick cure," and now she wanted Katy treated as previously planned. However, because of the time lapse and Katy's somewhat different stage of development, therapy plans were re–evaluated. Frances seemed quite patient with that process. She readily agreed to the new therapy plan, which included most of the elements of the original, including the lack of a promise that Katy would talk within a specified time.

As she and the program director talked about this plan, Frances said, "You and I both know I've wasted some time that Katy could have been getting help and I'm so sorry I did. I think I just needed something to work out all right *for me* right away. My whole life seemed pretty grim, my husband and then Katy, and all." The director, who had heard about Frances' shopping trips, had been quite annoyed with Frances when she first called and asked to come back to the center. However, as her discussion with Frances progressed, the professional felt increasing compassion for the woman and told her, "I guess this time has been hard on you, but you're here now and we'll pick up from here." As Katy's treatment progressed, Frances collaborated well with all the people involved.

Max, Marta, and Lori

Max and Marta were born and had grown up in a European country, and their three children were born there. Max owned a business of buying and selling antiques. He said his business had done very well in Europe but "not too good in this country where people don't appreciate really fine antiques." Marta said she had no desire to work outside the home, adding, "My job is taking care of Max and the girls and making a good home for my family."

When at 6 months old their youngest child, Lori, did not babble or turn to the sounds of their voices, Max took her to what he said was, "the finest hearing testing clinic in the country." There Lori was diagnosed as congenitally deaf. Unable to accept the diagnosis, Max closed up his business for two weeks and took Lori to "the finest clinic" in another European country. The same diagnosis of deafness was made.

Still unable to accept the diagnosis, and able to afford to do so, Max closed his business and moved his family to a city in the northeastern United States. He said he did so because he had heard from his relatives living there that "they had good testing facilities in the area."

Max and his family lived with these relatives and he said, "It was a bit crowded, but okay." Marta agreed it was crowded. Max opened a part-time antique business. He said this gave him "much less money but much more time to seek a satisfactory explanation of Lori's condition." He searched at several clinics and schools in the northeastern states but found no diagnosis more satisfactory to him.

Max and Marta were interviewed in a large southwestern city to which the family had moved because Max understood the university there provided "good help for children with hearing problems." Max again ran his business part-time. Lori, now almost 3 years old, was enrolled in the university program and also in a public school program for preschoolers with severe hearing impairment.

In the interview Max talked both for himself and for Marta. She seldom spoke except when asked a direct question. For example, when asked, Marta said she liked having a home of her own again. Then when the interviewer asked her how she felt about Lori, she started to reply, but Max answered quickly, "I am more upset about Lori's problems than she is, and her English isn't too good." Marta looked slightly annoyed. The interviewer said, "I'd like to hear what she has to say anyhow," and repeated the question to Marta. Marta replied, "My English *isn't* too good, but I want to stay here for Lori to be helped." When asked whether she thought Lori was indeed being helped, she responded vehemently, "Oh yes!"

The meaning of Marta's words perhaps was better understood later in the interview when Max said that, although he was happy with the university program, he was very unhappy with the public school training . He said, "Soon I'll have enough money for us to move to California where I understand the schools are better." The interviewer's inference was that Max was still "shopping," while Marta was ready to settle down where she felt Lori was getting help.

Commentary

Parents like Frances and Max who continue to seek a cure for their children can be extremely frustrating for professionals to work with and often stir resentment. Professionals who have done a careful diagnosis of the child and have planned a program of treatment have invested a great deal of time, effort, and care in the process. They may feel quite rejected when parents reject their work, or at least do not seem to respect it, by looking elsewhere for something better. Professionals are like all others: they want to feel trusted and may feel mistrusted by a parent who "shops" for additional opinions or therapy programs. Because the feeling of not being trusted is hurtful, it often leads to anger toward the parent.

An example of this reaction occurred in the case of Frances and Katy. The same personnel who had done the original evaluation and planning were called upon to do the re-evaluation and make the new plans, and several of them were the ones who would conduct Katy's treatment. The director of the rehabilitation program in which Katy was to be treated heard several of the professionals who were to work with the child make various remarks about how unfair Frances had been to Katy and to them, how arrogant she had been, and so forth. The director wisely called together all personnel who were to be involved with this family. In the meeting the director spoke of Frances' right to seek treatment she thought best for Katy, then acknowledged the frustration and resentment that the situation could cause for the professionals who had seen Katy previously.

After the director had listened to discussion of the emotions stirred up in the various professionals, she asked the professionals whether any of them had not at some time been faced with a situation that seemed so hard they just wished they could run away. Most of the group members nodded in the affirmative. The director then said, "This is just what Frances did. She ran away from a deeply frightening reality in the hope of making it go away or at least making it better quickly. It's our responsibility to let go of our feelings about her past behavior and do our best with her and Katy in the now." Of course, the feelings of some of the professionals did not immediately vanish, but the director's reminder of why Frances might have done what she did helped to stir compassion for her, so that Katy's treatment and Frances' role in it went more smoothly than it might have.

In the case of Max, some additional problems were experienced by the therapists and teachers. They not only felt that Max did not trust or respect them but they also were angered by his autocratic behavior. Lori's teacher was especially put out. She said angrily:

> I guess it's okay that in his culture men are the dominant ones, and it's certainly okay for him to question why I'm doing what I am with Lori. I like explaining what I do and why. It's the *way* he questions me that annoys me, like he's so superior and couldn't trust my reasoning on anything unless he can somehow check it out. Sometimes I feel he really dislikes all women, even his wife. I resent that, and I resent how he treats Marta. I try my best to keep reminding myself that his personality is what it is and I don't have to like it in order to do the best I can with Lori.

Professionals must *keep* reminding themselves that parents who search for a cure usually are reacting more to their situations than to the professionals or what the professionals have said or done. Of course, professionals must behave responsibly and in keeping with the best knowledge their specialities have to offer; but having done that, professionals cannot be responsible for parents' behavior.

We started this chapter by saying that parents probably "shop" to find a way to alleviate their pain, and earlier we said that a diagnosis of disability in a child can stir such extremely negative emotions that many parents try to deny the problem or retreat from it. These hypotheses seem verified in Max's case. In their discussion, the interviewer asked him, "Did you have Lori tested so many times because you thought the tests were poorly done?" He answered, "I could *not* believe *I* could have a deaf child. The other two hear well and there is no deafness in my family or hers (Marta's), so how it could be with Lori, I still don't know." Later in the interview, he also said he would advise professionals to listen to parents' hurt feelings, and the interviewer thought he was asking them to listen to *his* hurt feelings.

Some parents may have to run until they get through the denial stage and become able to both face their emotions and adapt to them. For example, a group of four mothers whose children were enrolled in a program for 2- and 3-year-olds who had severe hearing impairment asked for an appointment with the staff audiologist. They showed him an article from their local newspaper that announced a new experimental procedure for alleviating deafness and wanted their children referred for this surgery. One of the mothers said, "They just cut the nerve of hearing and the child can hear again." The audiologist realized that these women had no understanding of how hearing takes place, what the cochlear implant experimentation involved, or that the newest experimental procedure had been done only on older subjects. The audiologist explained all this as best he could to the mothers and tried to help them see how training could help their children. They listened attentively, and then one said, "I'm going to call that clinic today and find out whether they'll take our kids for this surgery and make them hear." The women returned several days later, crestfallen. One spoke for the group, "You were right, the surgery isn't for our kids. We just have to bite the bullet and keep training them and live with our impatience."

Some parents, like Max, may continue to cling to denial for a long time. These are the parents many professionals will see, but perhaps no professional will work with for very long. Perhaps when professionals listen with understanding to a Frances or Max, they will find a parent afraid to face the truth, and thus still living with denial, and their attitudes will be more compassionate and less resentful. Perhaps, also, when a professional can take the time to help such a troubled parent move beyond denial or retreat, that parent will "bite the bullet," experience the pain, and cease his or her shopping.

Suggested Readings

Buscaglia, L. (1975). *The disabled and their parents: A counseling challenge.* Thorofare, NJ: Charles B. Slack.

Gordon, S. (1988). *When living hurts.* New York: Dell.

CHAPTER FOUR

Guilt Takes Many Forms

As mentioned previously, parents of children with disabilities are very susceptible to feelings of guilt, which derive from many sources. When guilt is a pervasive emotion in parents, it profoundly affects behavior. Parents' guilt-driven behaviors in turn can cause difficulties for the professionals who work with them. In this chapter, we give examples that illustrate parents' guilt feelings and some of the behaviors professionals may have to cope with as a result of it. In the commentary, we examine some of the sources of guilt experienced by parents of children with disabilities, look briefly at the question of shame, and suggest some ways for professionals to deal with parents who carry a pervasive sense of guilt or shame.

Donna, Roy, and Bill

Donna grew up as one of five children, all girls, in a prominent, well-known family in a small Mississippi town. She often heard her mother and her mother's friends talking about how they pitied Donna's father, making comments such as, "Poor Carl, too bad he had no sons" and "men are so disappointed when they don't have a son." On several occasions Donna also heard both her parents discuss what a shame it was that there were no sons to carry on the family name.

As a child Donna felt that her parents' marriage was a troubled one, and this feeling got mixed up in her thinking with the feeling that her parents' trouble was caused by lack of sons in the family. She said that, even as an adult, she felt guilty that she could not have been a boy for her father's sake. Furthermore, she said something in her equated a successful marriage with having sons.

When Donna married Roy, who grew up in the same town and knew what people had said about her father and his family, she fervently hoped to have sons in her own family. She felt she must do so in order not to disappoint Roy as her father had been disappointed. Donna and Roy's first child was a girl; and Donna said she felt waves of guilt that she had let Roy down, "although he seemed very pleased with her." Her guilt intensified when a second daughter was born. She said she felt "so ashamed I couldn't produce a boy, and just desperate to have one."

Donna became pregnant again quite quickly, and finally, she and Roy had a son, whom they named Bill. She said, "I was overjoyed! Roy was pleased, too, but no more so than with the other children." Then she and Roy discovered Bill was born with multiple disabilities, including a malformed heart.

It wasn't until years later that Donna could talk about her feelings of guilt and shame with a support group. She said her initial reactions of shock and grief were compounded by her awful feelings of "failure about not being able to have a healthy son, particularly for Roy's sake."

She said that at that point she wasn't even thinking about things like the baby's need for heart surgery or what it would be like to rear him. "I just felt so guilty and kept thinking I could *not* face my parents with the news, so Roy took on the job of telling them about the baby." Donna said, "Roy told me that when he told them about Bill neither of my parents said a thing for a moment, then mother said, 'Oh, you poor thing!' Now Roy is pretty unflappable, but even he thought that was a pretty strange reaction."

Donna also reported that, once her parents knew that Bill had a disability, they "tried to ignore the whole situation, never asked how I felt or how Bill was, didn't come to the hospital when he had his three operations. They never offered any help until he was older and his heart was doing better. Roy worked in my father's office, so at least my father knew when Bill had his operations, but I felt *so* unloved when neither one of my parents made any attempt to help."

Donna participated in all of the recommended treatments for Bill. She said:

> I think I did all the things I was supposed to do in a haze of guilt and depression. And in fact I think those feelings might have made me too zealous in my efforts to help him. Several of his therapists told me I was trying too hard, doing his exercises too strenuously. They tried to help me relax a little so I wouldn't wear Bill out. And when they could get me to relax, which wasn't much of the time, I think I did better. At least I felt better.
>
> My guilt hasn't all gone away, though, because now it comes up again when I think my two older daughters were to some extent abandoned in my following up every resource for Bill, and I tried a number of treatments for him. Oh, I did all the usual mothering things for the girls, like seeing to their physical needs and getting them to and from their after school activities, but I know my mind was more on Bill and I was more involved with him.

Patricia, Kim, and John

Patricia was a very ambitious and upwardly mobile lawyer, as was her husband, John. Patricia was seen for an intake interview prior to enrolling Kim, who was then

2 years old and had cerebral palsy, for speech-language therapy. In the interview Patricia reported that when she was 34, she and John decided to have one child, thinking that her career was well enough established that she could be away from it for "three or four months." She said she felt "guilty and a little resentful" that she was less efficient during the last two months of her pregnancy, although she continued to work until three days before Kim's birth.

When asked about her reaction to Kim having cerebral palsy, Patricia said:

> I was appalled! I felt guilty that I had produced a deformed child. And I hated the idea of deformity, especially for a girl! I was angry, too, because I knew this was going to keep me away from my career longer than I had planned, and then I'd feel guilty that I didn't want to take care of my own child.

Asked whether she was now working full-time, she answered:

> Oh goodness, yes! I was off for eight months. Kim had digestive problems, and was just sick a lot, so I had to stay with her. I also had to take her for physical therapy, and all those examinations by an orthopedic surgeon. John and I also knew she didn't hear well and were sure she was retarded because she seemed so deformed.

When the interviewer said, "That must have been a hard time for you," Patricia said:

> I alternated between feeling resentful and feeling guilty. Resentful that I had to stay home with this

handicapped child while other lawyers were getting some of the cases I might have had. Then I'd get very guilty that I longed to be back at the office rather than at home with Kim. I knew as soon as I could find a reliable housekeeper, I'd have to go back to work to keep my sanity. Good housekeepers are hard to find, though, and I haven't yet had one I thoroughly trusted with Kim.

The speech-language pathologists who later worked with Kim said they saw Patricia only at the times scheduled for progress reports. Otherwise, a housekeeper brought the child for therapy. These professionals reported that in the year they had worked with the child, there had been three different housekeepers. They said all of the housekeepers felt Patricia didn't trust them, complaining that Patricia called them three or four times during a day to check on what they were doing and/or to remind them of the routine they said they already understood and were following. The professionals understood the housekeeper's feelings because they, too, received frequent phone calls from Patricia, questioning whether they were following the agreed-on therapy plan, whether they thought the plan should be changed, and so on.

The speech-language pathologists also said that Kim was making good progress in learning language, her gross motor skills were improving, and she was learning to play with other children. She seldom cried or seemed angry, except when it was time to leave the clinic, and they thought they understood her reluctance to go home: Patricia would not allow her to play outside except for short periods of time on warm days, nor could other children come to the house because Patricia thought Kim might catch an illness from them.

Commentary

There is hardly a parent who has escaped some sense of guilt over the course of rearing children. This is true partly because parenting is a very imprecise science and inevitably includes decisions and behaviors that later seem to have been in error. Furthermore, our culture tends to blame parents for their children's failure to live out cultural norms, even though the behavioral variance often is outside parents' legitimate control.

Given that the majority of young children with disabilities need an abundance of care and protection, their parents not only have the usual opportunities for guilt, but also often have an exaggerated sense of it. This overabundance of guilt can come from many sources. Sometimes it comes from a parent's own inner voice and sometimes from the voices of others. Patricia is an example of a mother whose guilt arose from her own inner conflicts. Donna's guilt probably was prompted by her early impressions from her own family.

The following statements are typical of comments we have heard from parents that reflect both inner and outer stimuli for guilt:

"I must have done something wrong to deserve this."

"I believe God is punishing me because I really didn't want another child."

"My doctor told me not to gain weight, but my mother says I didn't eat enough for two and that's why the baby was so premature."

"I often didn't rest when I was dog-tired and this may have affected my baby."

"My husband says our child's retardation had to come from my side of the family because there were no problems in his family and I did have a cousin with this condition."

These statements will probably not make sense to professionals unless they understand how guilt functions in human life.

Possible Factors in Guilt

The problem of understanding guilt is compounded in many ways. First, there seem to be two types of guilt. Horney (1965) made a distinction between what she called "Real Guilt" and "Phony Guilt." Her point was that real guilt arises when a person knows he or she has wronged another person. This guilt is characterized by an attempt, if possible, to right the wrong. On the other hand, phony guilt acts to displace other emotions (i.e., it serves as a substitute for such emotions as anger or fear). For example, it may have seemed easier to Donna to feel guilty about not having a son than to acknowledge, and feel, her deep anger at her parents for their attitudes about girls. In any case, although phony guilt feels very real to the person experiencing it, it usually is not supported by any wrong-doing.

Karen (1992) raised another point to be considered in professionals' attempts to understand parents' behaviors. Karen, whose research has been on the subject of shame, distinguished between the emotions of guilt and shame. Karen maintained that human beings experience both emotions, guilt being the perception of having wronged another person, shame being the emotion of not liking (being ashamed of) oneself. As Karen wrote about the subject, he pointed out that guilt is linked to knowing that one has behaved in a way that harmed another, but shame is the feeling of not being good enough. Lewis (1992) agreed that shame is the pervasive feeling of dislike for oneself.

In the thinking of Karen and Lewis, shame is a more basic emotion than guilt. These authors gave examples of ways in which parents make children feel ashamed and how such shame gnaws at children as they mature. Those feelings of shame, acquired in early childhood, are then carried into adulthood and influence adult behavior.

A woman we worked with exemplified what Karen discussed as shame. She was a petite young woman from a prominent family in a small town. Known for her beautiful figure, while she was in college she was a cheerleader, a member of a well-thought-of sorority, and a beauty queen. She then married a prominent attorney from the same town. Their three-year marriage had not gone smoothly, and they had separated once and then reconciled. The woman said later that when she married this man, "It got a lot of tongues wagging in our town. He was known to be a brilliant man but a large drinker with an even larger ego. Some people thought he must have been drunk to marry me."

When she became pregnant, she did not want anyone to know about it, not even her husband. She wore heavy corsets all during her seven months of pregnancy and gained so little weight that even the people she saw most often were unaware that she was pregnant. Her husband (who slept in a separate bed) was flabbergasted when he discovered her pregnancy only a few weeks before she delivered a very premature daughter. The baby was severely brain damaged and had heart and liver malfunction, but she lived for four years. As professionals worked with the child, the woman often excused herself from treatment sessions, saying, "I'm sorry, but I just can't help now, knowing I caused this." After the mother had made this comment several times, a professional asked her why she thought she was the cause of the child's problems. The mother told the professional about her corsets, failure to eat properly while pregnant, and heavy drinking at the parties she and her husband continued to attend until the night the baby was born. The professional said, "It must have been *so* important to you to keep your pregnancy a secret. Do you know why that was?" The woman, in tears, said, "Oh yes, my husband needed status and recognition so badly, and, after all, all I had going for me was my figure."

A statement like this woman made suggests she did not like herself as a total human being, and struggled with being ashamed of who and what she was. However, as Karen emphasized, it is hard to tell whether guilt or shame, or both, are operative at any given moment. We will continue to refer to guilt here because it is a familiar term. Nevertheless, professionals should recognize that some of parents' statements about what they have done wrong probably are telling more about their feelings of shame than actual wrong-doing.

Professionals need to consider another possible factor in parents' guilt. As Samalin (1991) has pointed out, from time to time most parents get angry with their children and then feel very guilty about having done so. Likewise, parents of children with disabilities will feel anger toward them, with subsequent guilt. Parents of children with disabilities also may get stuck in unresolved early stages of crisis reaction, as delineated in Chapter 1, and may still feel resentment and anger about having such a child. Certainly children with disabilities place restrictions and requirements on parents that can stir what can be thought of as "existential anger" or "life anger." When this is the case, parents can feel terribly guilty about their anger. Patricia's guilt seems to be a particularly characteristic example of this problem.

Behaviors Arising from Guilt

A troublesome form that parents' guilt sometimes takes is overprotectiveness of the child. It is as if these parents fear that if they are not overly careful they could be the cause of harm to their children. It also is possible that overprotectiveness can be a characteristic of parents whose guilt stems from repressed anger and resentment. Such anger, and its related guilt and mistrust, can be projected onto the professionals who work with the child, as if the parent were saying, "If I can't be trusted to do the right thing for my child, certainly no professional can unless I keep them on a tight leash."

Related to the overprotection issue but also somewhat different is the overloving, overgiving parent. An example of overgiving is the young mother who said, "I have dedicated my life to this little girl." She was unwilling to leave the child with anyone else, including competent family members, because she insisted that only she could care for the child.

Sometimes parents' overdoing takes the form of trying to do more than is prescribed or necessary for their children. A woman who kept asking the physical therapist for more exercises to do with her son is a case in point. The therapist explained several times that the number of exercises and duration of the exercise plan the woman had been given were sufficient. When the mother kept pressing to be given more, the therapist, who was beginning to feel annoyed, asked the woman why she could not be satisfied with doing what she had been asked to do. The woman talked about the terrible guilt she felt that she had somehow injured her child, and her thinking that if she worked extra hard to train the boy, she might partially make it up to him. The therapist then tried to help the mother see that she was doing all that could be done in therapy for her son and was doing a good job with what was necessary. However, this mother never did seem to relax with the amount she was doing.

In most cases, a parent's wish to do more in training is not harmful to the child, as was the case in the last example. Nevertheless, there are cases in which a parent's guilt-driven overdoing can be harmful. Donna, in an earlier example, had said she was too zealous in trying to help her son, Bill, who had a serious heart problem. She gave the following example of what she meant by "too zealous." The cardiologist who treated Bill after his several surgeries told Donna to take Bill out for a short walk every day; he specified that it should be no more than a 15 minute walk to start out. Donna reported that she thought if 15 minutes was good, longer might be better. Consequently, the next time she took Bill to the cardiologist, she reported proudly that she and Bill walked almost every day for half an hour. The cardiologist was, as Donna reported it, "furious," telling her that she could damage Bill's heart from putting too much stress on it. Donna said the doctor's reaction "didn't do a thing for my guilt, but it sure made me walk Bill only 15 minutes a day."

Some parents who devote their lives to their children with disabilities appear to play the role of victims. For example, a mother who said she had devoted her life to her child also reported that her marriage had been in trouble for several years and she had hoped a baby would make it more tolerable. The child was born with fingers attached to small stumps of arms. The woman devoted all of her time and attention to the baby, refusing to let others care for the child so that she might go out with her husband and refusing to spend time at home with him. She said later, "I guess spending all my time with the baby was a way of getting back at him (husband); and why not, when I was stuck in a rotten marriage and didn't have even the satisfaction of producing a healthy child?" Only later, and with the help of counseling, did she see that she was playing the role of a helpless martyr. She also began to see that her insistence on enacting this victim or martyr role made it difficult for those who tried to help her take constructive steps for the benefit of herself and her child.

In contrast to the overdoing, overgiving pattern, professionals sometimes see a pattern of parent withdrawal. For example, one mother in a well-to-do family reported that she simply was unable to manage her son with cerebral palsy. She said it was fortunate that the family could afford full-time home care for the boy because she " fell apart" when she saw him struggle to learn simple motor tasks. Each time she tried to help with him she thought, "I have done this to him by birthing him." Thus she abdicated all responsibility for his care and training, turning his care over to others to keep herself from confronting her feelings of guilt and pain.

Some Thoughts for Professionals

Although many parents of children with disabilities cope quite constructively with most of their inevitable feelings of guilt, it seems they must struggle with these feelings over and over again. One message for professionals is that, whatever form their guilt may take, parents need understanding, support, and opportunities to explore and clarify their feelings. Otherwise, these feelings may undermine the more positive emotions and behaviors necessary in treatment of their children. These feelings also can negatively affect how well professionals assist in providing opportunities to the child and his or her parents.

Another message is that professionals can behave in ways that increase parents' guilt. For example, a speech-language pathologist was known to ask a mother why she waited so long to start treatment for her child. Again, a preschool teacher often told parents they were making mistakes, saying in a stern voice things such as, "Oh, no, you should *never* do that!" Parents do not need to be coddled, but neither do they benefit or change by being scolded. Professionals should monitor their communication so that they avoid sending parents on yet another guilt trip.

In the real world of professional practice, most personnel cannot spend as much time as they'd like to in interaction with parents. Most professionals must assist parents in context of their duties with children. However, lack of time is no excuse for giving little help or poor help to parents. The main reason some professionals slight parents and family members seems to be one of focus; these professionals often focus almost exclusively on children and children's difficulties.

Professionals who can enlarge their focus to see each child in the context of his or her family will provide time for helping parents and other family members involved with the child. The more family centered view is an accurate one because, just as each child is unique, he or she lives in a unique family situation that inevitably influences his or her development.

We encourage all professionals to adopt a more family centered approach to their work. Those who do so will be aware of and understand that emotions such as guilt, shame, and anger in parents and family members potentially inhibit their effective collaboration with professionals. Such professionals will attempt to make their time with parents and/or family members as productive as possible. They will understand the response of a psychologist who spoke to the issue of time when he lectured on parent counseling to a large convention audience. A woman challenged him, saying, "It's easy for you to talk about all these important ways we can help parents. You have an hour with them, probably once a week. I'm lucky if I get 15 minutes a week with the parents whose children I work with." The psychologist said kindly, "I know that's a disadvantage, so I can only say to you, 'If you have 15 minutes, then try to make it the best 15 minutes you have to give.'" In whatever time professionals have with parents, awareness of and greater understanding about emotions such as guilt inevitably will influence the ways they relate and talk to parents, and will make a difference in how parents feel.

Suggested Readings

Horney, K. (1965). *The neurotic personality of our time.* New York: W. W. Norton.

Karen, R. (1992). Shame. *The Atlantic, 269*(2), 40–70.

Lewis, M. (1992). *Shame: The exposed self.* New York: The Free Press.

Wilcox, M. (in press). Enhancing initial communication skills in young children with developmental disabilities through partner programming. *Seminars in Speech and Hearing.*

CHAPTER FIVE

Parents Need Confirmation

B ecause of the emotional upheavals and the stress parents experience in caring for their children with disabilities, many of them have a diminished sense of their own self-worth. They need to feel that they are respected for who they are as well as what they do. They also need to be reinforced for what they do well. Whether or not other family members provide such confirmation, professionals certainly can do so. The following examples illustrate two cases, one in which the parents did *not* receive such confirmation and one in which they did.

Jane, Jack, and Gary

Gary was born to Jane and Jack at a time and in a hospital in which fathers were not allowed in the delivery room and mothers were heavily sedated, so neither one knew his condition at birth. Jane, still groggy, and Jack were in Jane's room waiting for the baby to be brought in when the obstetrician who delivered Gary arrived instead. They were aghast when the doctor told them Gary had Down syndrome. He said the child would be severely mentally and motorically retarded and probably wouldn't live to adulthood. According to Jane's report of the encounter, in "practically the same sentence" in which the doctor gave the diagnosis, he advised them not to take Gary home but to institutionalize him immediately and offered to sign the necessary papers. Jane said both she and Jack felt the doctor's presentation was "cruel," and they demanded to see the baby.

When Gary was brought to them, Jack, who had never seen an infant with this disorder, was particularly shocked and distressed. Jane said he "spent the afternoon thinking the doctor was right, that immediate institutionalization was best, that they could never live with such a child." Jane was "extremely disappointed, too, and sorry for Jack that his son was this way." However, Jane was adamant that they should take the baby home and try to care for him, saying "we talked and cried long into that night till I fell asleep." The next day Jack reluctantly agreed with Jane that they would indeed take Gary home and see how they got along with managing him before acting on the obstetrician's advice.

The first time we talked with Jane, her son, Gary, was with her. He was 4 years old and went three mornings a week with her to the Head Start program where she worked part-time. He appeared to be a docile, friendly, smiling child, and Jane said he seemed well liked and included by the other children. Gary's ability to mix with other children was borne out when he went willingly to a playroom and played happily with the other children while we talked with Jane.

Jane reported that the early years with Gary were rough ones. She said that she and Jack had some real conflicts about how the boy should be managed, and Jack often got depressed about Gary's slowness. She declared angrily, "Worst of all was the grief we got from my parents. They thought we were crazy to try to raise him at home, and said so every chance they got."

Jane told of incidents in which her mother had seen Gary misbehave and made comments to Jane that were some variation on her repetitious theme of "I told you that you couldn't do it," and her father just refused to relate to Gary no matter how much Gary went to him. She said her parents' behaviors hurt her deeply.

> I just felt abandoned at a time I needed them so much. Their rejection also made Jack and me furious and even more stubborn. Besides, we both were growing to love Gary and to get real pleasure from his sunny disposition.

Gary doesn't go to my mother and father now like he tried to when he was younger; I guess he feels they don't like him much, and he's right. But he knows we love him, even when we get mad at him, and he's even more delightful now that he's beginning to develop a sense of humor. My parents don't see that side of him, only his appearance, clumsiness, his slow speech, and his retardation.

When asked whether she had to see her parents often, Jane said:

Too often to suit me; they live only a couple of blocks away so my mother comes in sometimes on days I'm not working. My sister and brother and their families also live in town, and the pattern was for the whole family to get together at my parents for holidays and birthdays; but since Gary's second birthday when we were so uncomfortable, Jack and I have begged off and not gone. My sister-in-law is okay; at least she doesn't act like Gary is a freak and I'm an idiot to keep him home. Of course, I feel I can't call on my parents for any kind of help, but when Gary's sick on days I have to work I call my sister or sister-in-law or a friend to look after him.

When we last talked at length with Jane, Gary was 12 and in a class for children with developmental disabilities. Jane said Gary had a hard time learning school work, but he had learned basic skills of living and was reading on a second-grade level. She chuckled when she said, "He can make change for a dollar, but a five or ten is beyond him." She smiled proudly when she added, "He has a real gift for getting along with people, and he gives both Jack and me so much pleasure, we know we did the right thing in spite of the doctor and my parents."

Sharon, Doug, and Jill

Before Sharon and Doug (Chapter 1) brought their daughter, Jill, home after five months in the neonatal critical care unit, the hospital staff pediatrician had a conference with them in which he explained the various types of care that Jill would need. He told them that because she still had intermittent congestion in her lungs she would be sent home with an oxygen machine and would probably continue to need oxygen for a couple of months, but that her need for it should decrease fairly rapidly over that time. The doctor assured them that before he discharged her, she needed the machine only for about half an hour and only when she started wheezing, which had been about every five hours. The doctor suggested that they set the alarm for five hours during the night so they could sleep in between Jill's treatments. He also explained that the breathing tube would need cleaning after several uses and showed them the cleaning procedure.

However, the first night Jill was home Sharon was so nervous that Jill would start wheezing that she intended to keep her on the machine all night. Then she became anxious about the tube becoming clogged so that she "cleaned it out just about every hour." This awakened Jill, who then moaned and whimpered and stayed awake. Unsure of what to do for her, Sharon tried to hold her and rock her to sleep. Sharon said:

this was a bad mistake. She just got stiff and moaned like I was hurting her. I got Doug up and he was so damned reasonable, it made me furious, telling me they wouldn't have sent her home with the instructions they gave us if she was going to clog up every hour. But I knew Doug was right so I put Jill back in her crib and I sat beside her and patted her till she went back to sleep. I set the alarm for five hours, then stayed awake listening for it to ring, cleaned her up again, and did like I had done before, patting her till she went back to sleep.

The next day I called the pediatrician at the critical care unit and told him what we'd done. He was so patient with me, said he understood I'd be nervous, but said we'd done the right thing not to bother her except every five hours and not to clean the tube so often. He also suggested I try to sleep for those hours because I needed to get rest, too. He said to check the five-hour schedule in the daytime to see if that was often enough and that I could call him if that schedule didn't seem to be okay, or if Jill ran into any kind of trouble. I can't tell you how much it meant to feel I could do something he thought was right and to have his support.

Commentary

Professionals who work with young children with disabilities must keep in mind that their parents and other family members suffer deprivation. Parents are deprived of a major satisfaction that comes with the difficult job of parenting; that is, the satisfaction of watching their children develop in ways that are age-appropriate. Other family members, too, may feel helpless as these children are slow to develop and may not know how best to react to them.

Parents and families may wait anxiously for a long time before they get the reinforcement of a verbal response from the child. It is well known, for example, that parents of young children with severe hearing impairment talk less and less to them as the children fail to verbalize in return (Simmons-Martin, 1976). These parents can quickly learn to continue talking to their children when someone helps them understand the importance of verbal stimulation, even when they receive minimal feedback. Again, a child's slow motor development may be a factor that provokes questions and comments from others. One woman reported that one of her neighbors asked her whether she thought her son would ever be able to walk and all she could say was, "I pray he will, but then the very next time she saw me she asked me again when I thought he'd walk." In other cases, a child's physical problems may actually interfere with normal adult-child physical interaction, such as a grandmother's reported fear of hurting her grandson by picking him up and holding him on her lap, or a mother's anxiety about feeding her child who had problems with swallowing.

Professionals Can Appreciate and Reinforce Parents

In professionals' concern for treating children who have disabilities, it is sometimes easy to overlook their parents' needs, not only for training, but also for reinforcement for some things they are doing very well in their incredibly demanding roles. Often other family members provide such reinforcement; but whether family members are supportive or not, it is still imperative for parents to feel reinforced by the professionals with whom they work. As one woman put it, "My mother tells me I'm really helping Jim learn, but my mother has been on my side all along; it really means more to me when Jim's teacher tells me that."

Professionals sometimes will need to search for parent behaviors they feel are commendable, and will need to be able to describe such behaviors. Continuing reinforcement is needed by everyone who is learning new skills, techniques, or approaches. It is important that such expressions of appreciation and reinforcement begin with the first professional-parent encounter. For example, the examiner of an 18-month-old boy told his parents who wanted him to have a speech and language evaluation, "He's a lucky little boy to have parents who know that he needs to have help early."

Parents' Learning May Proceed Slowly

Throughout a child's treatment his or her parents receive many suggestions and recommendations from each of the specialists working with them. They are given many new and different things to do. Throughout the learning of new things, it is very meaningful to parents to have professionals communicate their awareness of the fact that there are many things parents *have done* and *are doing* that are positive and helpful to the child.

It also is important for each specialist to remember that the learning of any new skill is seldom done all at once. Rather, learning usually takes place in incremental steps (i.e., in successive approximations toward the goal of mastering the skill). Reinforcement for each level of improvement helps to ensure that the next level will be obtained.

It is *not* desirable to tell parents that they did something right when in fact it was not done correctly. Parents can spot an insincere compliment and will resent it.

Instead, professionals can assist parents' learning with comments such as, "That's better than last time you tried (specifying the procedure)," or "You got that part of it just right, now let's try the next part."

Professionals' words of commendation to parents and other family members should be not only sincere, but also specific. The person being commended should be told exactly what he or she has done right or is doing better. These behaviors were exemplified by a home health nurse whose job included teaching mothers how to feed their babies with cleft palates prior to the time the infants' palates were repaired. The nurse reported that most of the women were terrified that their babies would choke when fed. The nurse first taught each mother how to hold the infant so milk would be less likely to go up into the nose, a fairly easy task to learn. She could then say sincerely to the mother, "Good, you're holding the baby just right and that's at least half of the job." As the mother gave the baby the bottle, the nurse encouraged her with such phrases as, "You're doing well not to tip the bottle too high," and "O.K.! More of it got swallowed that time!" Such simple reinforcement helped the mothers to relax, to learn more quickly, and to feel successful. Incidentally, the nurse's manner of teaching also kept her very much in demand.

Helping Parents Appreciate Their Children

In addition to feeling satisfaction for their own positive behaviors, parents of children with disabilities often need to be helped to feel satisfaction with their children's accomplishments, however slowly they may come along. Professionals can help in this regard by pointing out a child's improvements and noting that each one is something the parent can feel good about. This support can be given in such a way that it helps parents retain realistic satisfaction rather than building up false hopes.

A similar problem encountered with many parents is their inability to appreciate the unique qualities their children possess beyond the given disability. All human beings tend to develop perceptual sets that can "filter out" the good qualities of another person. Likewise, some parents can have perceptual sets that filter out awareness of, and delight in, their children's uniquely good qualities. Jane and Jack, the parents of the boy in our earlier example, were parents who could appreciate their child's good qualities. From Jane's accounts, her parents (the boy's grandparents) seemed to exemplify people who overlooked the good qualities.

Parental perceptions probably have been shaped by the demands life has placed on them in caring for their children. Furthermore, whether or not professionals intend to do so, and whether or not they like the idea, professionals strongly influence parents' perceptions of their children. Certainly much of parents' time with professionals is spent talking about or working on problems, and in most cases less of the professional's attention is given to helping parents feel delight in some aspect of their children. For example, when parents meeting in a discussion group were asked what they *liked* about their children, several said they hadn't ever talked or thought much about that, and several others said they couldn't think of a thing. However, one woman, whose daughter could only raise and turn her head as she lay in the prone position, said, "If it counts as an answer, I love it when she lifts her head and smiles at me." The group leader assured the mother that her daughter's smiles were a wonderful part of her and to be treasured. Several other parents looked thoughtful, and one said, "I think we'd all be better off if we could take more notice of things like that."

When professionals notice positive qualities in children, they need to call parents' attention to them. For example, parents can be reminded of their child's determination to live and develop, or of his or her amiable acceptance of treatment, and so forth. Remember, in the previous example, it was the physical therapist who first pointed out to Jane and Jack that their son, Gary, was friendly and seemed to have a "sunny" disposition.

An example of a professional who helped parents appreciate the uniqueness of a child was the teacher of a 3-year-old girl with severe hearing impairment. The teacher noticed that when the child could pick up the beat of music, she danced very gracefully. The teacher asked the child's mother whether she had noticed this. The mother had not, but agreed to play music at home to give the child opportunities to dance. Watching the child dance became a source of pleasure for her family. The little girl loved their attention and applause, and she was even more thrilled when another family member would dance with her. This girl later danced in elementary and high school plays, much to her family's delight and pride.

Professionals must not overlook the joy and laughter that some children with disabilities can bring into a family. As another example, Jeff, a 4-year-old, wore two hearing aids and was attending an oral school, but he relied mainly on signing unless reminded to try to speak. One day he signed to his mother that he was going to teach his grandmother, who was extremely deaf, to use signs. About an hour later he came to his mother with his head bowed in discouragement. When asked what was wrong, Jeff signed, "Granny can't learn." When his mother asked why, Jeff signed, "She just won't listen." When Jeff's mother told his father about the incident, they shared both amusement and pleasure that Frank cared about being able to communicate with his grand-mother. Frank's teacher was also amused when she heard the story, and she pointed out to his mother that Jeff was also sensitive to others in the classroom.

Parents Working in Groups Can Support Each Other

Although working with groups of parents is not feasible in all professional settings, in many settings it is possible to do so. For example, preschool special educators and educational audiologists working with young children with hearing impairments have found that seeing groups of parents of the children in their programs is an efficient way to provide information that is pertinent to all of them.

Provision of information, however, is only one reason for group work with parents. If allowed to do so during the group meeting time, parents can support and confirm each other. They also can make suggestions to each other, often more effectively than a professional can; that is, a bond can grow between parents because they struggle with similar issues in rearing their children.

When professionals think about working with groups of parents, it is helpful to remember that parents of children with various disabilities face similar issues. The similarity in parents' concerns means that professionals can group together parents of children with very different disabilities. For example, Frank, the single parent referred to earlier, whose son, Taylor, had cerebral palsy, was in a group with Mary, the 62-year-old grandmother rearing her granddaughter who had Down syndrome; Jean, the mother of a child whose hyperactivity was not yet completely controlled medically; and Sandy, the mother whose 3-year-old son had acquired paraplegia in a car accident in which her husband was killed. This group met for six sessions of an hour each. The group leader started each session with some information about the children's various programs and answered the participants' questions. Then the participants discussed issues that were currently important to them, crises that had arisen, and their current feelings about themselves and their children.

Group members shared some of their sad feelings, and even Frank had tears in his eyes as he told of his feelings when his wife left him shortly after Taylor was born, saying she couldn't handle living with such a child. The women in the group were irate about Frank's wife, but after a few minutes of venting their anger, Sandy said, "No use us being mad at her, she's gone; it's Frank we need to care about." The others agreed, tried to comfort Frank, and commended him for the job he was doing running his business and still taking care of his boy.

Members of the group also shared in the joy when good news was reported. For example, one morning Sandy announced proudly that her son was now strong enough to pull himself up on the bars, so he was on his way to having the strength to handle crutches. Mary exclaimed, "He'll be a Rocky by the time he's 4, then what will you do?"

Groups such as this seem to mean a great deal to people who have experienced them, many of whom have reported the group gave them their first chance to talk with other people who would know how they felt. For example, as the last meeting of his group was drawing to a close, Frank's beeper went off. As he stood up to leave to call his office, he told the others he wanted them to know they had helped him a lot. He said that at first he

felt strange being the only man, and had felt embar-
rassed when Jean said, "Good, now we can get a man's
point of view," "because I didn't know whether I'd have
anything to say." He went on, "But you teased me about
avoiding the group that first day my beeper kept going
off, and I loved that. You're the first people I could ever
really talk with about my wife—guys in bars aren't much
help—and you helped me learn to have more fun with
Taylor." He looked around the room, said simply, "I
thank you" and left the room.

Conducting groups is a very challenging and
demanding professional activity, if only because the
group leader must be aware of the needs of all the people
in the group. The leader must ensure that all participants have chances to talk. This means the leader must
be aware of people who look as if they wish to come into
the discussion, must ensure that one person does not
dominate the discussion time, and when interruptions
occur, must see that the discussion returns to the point
being made by the original speaker. Participants may
come from diverse cultural backgrounds, and the leader
may have to help them understand each other. There are
also times when the leader must deal creatively with
arguments between participants.

For all of these reasons, some professionals who otherwise could conduct group meetings that are more than
collective information-giving sessions may feel insecure
in initiating such groups. Many of these professionals,
however, already have the communication skills essential
to the task. For example, they are able to listen actively;
they are comfortable with silence as well as with talking;
and they understand the importance of turn-taking. Professionals also will gain experience as they participate in
these groups. Professionals who do engage in group work

with parents will find it a very meaningful part of their practice.

Summary

In this chapter, we have tried to remind professionals that, of all the very important things they do for parents, none may be more important than: (a) confirming parents as people of worth; (b) commending parents' efforts while reinforcing their accomplishments; and (c) helping them find sources of satisfaction in their children as unique human beings who also have disabilities.

Suggested Readings

Bates, M., & Johnson, C. (1972). *Group leadership: A manual for group counseling leaders.* Denver, CO: Love Publishing.

Luterman, D. (1979). *Counseling parents of hearing-impaired children.* Boston: Little, Brown.

Luterman, D. (1991). *Counseling the communicatively disordered and their families.* Austin, TX: PRO-ED.

Rollin, W. (1987). *The psychology of communication disorders in individuals and their families* (pp. 176-179). Englewood Cliffs, NJ: Prentice-Hall.

Webster, E. (1989). Parent counseling: One more challenge. *The Clinical Connection, 3*(4) 1-3.

CHAPTER SIX

Continuing Professional Dilemmas

M ost professionals who work with young children with disabilities have had considerable experience in dealing with a wide variety of personalities. However, despite professionals' best efforts, they will continue to face emotional responses in parents (and in themselves) that will challenge their own emotions, attitudes, and behaviors. As human beings, professionals bring their own needs, fears, crises, and points of vulnerability to their encounters with parents. Therefore, to establish and maintain quality parent-professional collaboration, they must face their own as well as parents' reactions.

There are certain conditions that professionals experience sooner or later as dilemmas in the complex business of human interaction. The way in which professionals manage these conditions can have profound effects on their constructive collaboration with parents. This chapter addresses common issues that represent potential sources of dilemma and, therefore, of stress.

Defensiveness

An attitude of defensiveness is one of the most common barriers to constructive communication and cooperative endeavor. Defensiveness is a very human response of needing to protect oneself in the face of some degree of threat to one's personal (or professional) self-image. Since few, if any, persons are invulnerable to such threats, it is an issue to be dealt with in all interactions. Of particular importance here, defensiveness must be dealt with in that particular human equation which is parent-professional collaboration in helping children with disabilities.

In many interactions between a parent and a professional, the threat to either's self-image may be minimal and therefore produce only minor behavioral patterns of defensiveness, for example, a quiet withdrawal. On the other hand, defensiveness may be expressed as strongly as a direct personal attack on the other person, which may be seen by the person being attacked as unprovoked aggression. In either case, defensiveness is a force that reduces or destroys openness and trust in interpersonal communication. Patton and Giffin (1981) reported studies of defensive behavior and discussed at length ways defensiveness functions to limit the effectiveness of human interaction. Much of the supportive data for the present discussion is adapted from these studies. Understanding how defensiveness works can help professionals cope with their own and parents' feelings of defensiveness and the behaviors that stem from these feelings.

Defensiveness breeds defensiveness. It is perhaps impossible for professionals not to feel defensive under certain conditions, such as when a parent refuses recommended treatment or questions the wisdom of procedures the specialist is using. It is further unlikely that any professional will avoid encountering defensive attitudes in some parents. The next section contains a discussion of three situations in which defensiveness and its management can play a significant role.

Confrontation, Conflict, and Negotiation

These three aspects of communication are grouped together because they often occur in the same encounter. They also can be among the most challenging situations of professional practice. Many people try to avoid confronting others about certain issues where they expect conflict. This avoidance happens because the confronter fears he or she can't handle the conflict. People also delay confrontation until their own emotions (e.g., fear or anger), are so strong that they justifiably fear they will stir a strong emotional response from the person being confronted. Such avoidance or delay is unfortunate because through negotiation, designed to reduce defensiveness, most conflicts can be handled constructively.

Although there probably are many situations in which professionals confront parents, there are three situations in which parents inevitably must be confronted with information. First, they must be told the diagnostic findings. Second, they must be given the recommendations for the treatment plan and sites of treatment. Third, parents' potential roles in treatment and follow-up must be described.

Of course, many, or perhaps even most, confrontations go smoothly and without conflict. However, each type of information has the potential to stir conflict with its attendant defensiveness. Thus, each of these situations can present a strong challenge to professionals' communication skills.

When conflict results from confrontations like those just described, or in any other situation, it means that the confrontation has stirred some degree of threat. For example, the diagnostic findings may refute parents' denial of the severity of their child's disability, or a recommendation may challenge a parent's previously held values and priorities. Another source of threat to parents may be the amount of parent involvement that is recommended in the treatment plan. For some parents, a very active role in treatment may seem overwhelming and dash their previous hopes that the professionals would do it all. Other parents may have hoped to have a much more active role in their children's treatment than is recommended, at least for the present, and may feel their needs to be highly involved have been violated.

In the face of a perceived threat, whatever its cause, parents usually feel defensive. As stated previously, defensiveness can take many forms, from quiet withdrawal to highly emotional expressions of shock and anger. In cases in which the parent expresses shock or anger outwardly, he or she may disagree vehemently with the diagnosis or treatment plan, state angrily that the treatment plan is unworkable, or belittle the professional talking with him or her. Such parental behaviors in turn can stir defensiveness in the professional and lead to further conflict. Two examples of conflict follow.

An unanticipated parental reaction that taxed an audiologist's communication skills occurred when a woman brought her 2-year-old daughter for a hearing evaluation. After careful audiometric testing and observing the child's responses to speech in a free-field situation, the audiologist reported to the mother what he thought would be good news: The little girl's hearing was normal. As the audiologist told of the incident, he said, "I thought that mother would be overjoyed, but she was furious, questioned whether my equipment was any good, and asked how much experience I had in testing children this young. Before I could answer her question about my experience, she told me she'd have to find a more qualified tester." The audiologist said that when he had recovered sufficiently from the woman's attack, he attempted to clarify her response. He said to her, "I'm surprised that you really seem disappointed that your little girl isn't deaf. Can you tell me why?" He reported that at that point the woman broke down and sobbed, "I knew something was wrong and I thought she must be either deaf or retarded. I thought I could cope with deafness because she could be trained and really accomplish some things. I just don't know how I can stand a retarded child!" The audiologist listened to her fears about retardation, then suggested that there might be some other causes for the child's lack of attention and unresponsiveness. He told the woman he was not qualified to test for conditions other than problems with hearing, but would be glad to send his report to any other center that could give the little girl a battery of tests for various problems. He then suggested several such centers. He told the mother that if the child did turn out to have learning problems, he thought she would need some help in coping with her feelings about the child and her situation. The audiologist also told the woman that there were support groups for parents of children with various types of disorders. The audiologist said the woman seemed to accept the notion that there might be causes other than deafness or retardation for her child's behavior, and seemed to accept his referral for more testing. He said she dried her eyes, took the list of possible test locations, and commented with a smile when she left, "You're right, if she's retarded, *I'll* need a lot of help."

A case of conflict of values and priorities occurred between a speech-language pathologist and Ken and Lois, the wealthy parents of a 3-year-old boy, Jerry. Jerry had been diagnosed as having minimal cerebral dysfunction with hyperactivity. The speech-language pathologist recommended that the boy be enrolled in a preschool program for children with neurological impairment who had difficulty with learning language. The professional described the program as one in which children were seen in small groups as well as individually, and the emphasis was on language learning.

The child's father interrupted further discussion to say, "I can afford to pay for all the individual training my son will need, and I will *not* have him in any special groups where he's thrown with children who are so much worse off than he is! He can't be comfortable there! If your program can't treat him individually, we'll find a place that can."

The speech-language pathologist replied, "Of course you have the right to select the training for him. Our clinic can provide individual work, and if that's what you choose, we can do that, but I really believe he would benefit from the group experience as well." She asked whether the parents would be willing, while the boy had individual training, to watch the group for several sessions with the professional there to explain the reason for certain of the activities, before deciding that it was not right for their son. The boy's mother thought this was a good idea, and the professional and parents negotiated this compromise. As it turned out, after observing the group for several sessions, the parents asked that their son be enrolled in the group the next time there was an opening.

As the examples just given show, resolution of conflict between parents and professionals requires sensitive negotiation to expedite outcomes that are in keeping with parents' rights and with their children's best interests. Because professionals' application of principles of constructive communication is crucial to the management of these situations, these principles are reviewed briefly here.

Principles of Constructive Communication

In the course of living, people learn various patterns of communication and recognize that these patterns exert a strong influence on their relationships with other people, sometimes for better and sometimes for worse. For example, some people learn that silence can be a powerful weapon, or that sarcasm can express a criticism but allow the speaker to say, if confronted, "Oh, I was just teasing." Of course, many people also learn more effective ways of expressing their reactions, and some of these ways will be discussed next.

Probably none of the following principles of constructive communication will seem entirely new to any reader. The ideas are relatively simple. Their execution is not!

Review of these principles and increased awareness of them can be helpful in two ways. First, they can help professionals improve skills in achieving the outcomes they desire in their relationships with parents. Second, the principles provide a way to help professionals analyze their successes with parents, as well as their mistakes, as they look back on previous encounters.

Using Description, Inference, and Judgment Appropriately

Most professionals are careful to differentiate between these three types of statements and use them appropriately in their written reports. They must use the same caution when talking with parents.

Description reports information that can be verified (i.e., facts such as test scores or what a person said or did). Because they report verifiable information, descriptive statements promote the highest level of agreement.

Inferences are hypotheses or statements of probability based on descriptive data (e. g., "Our findings suggest the possibility of neurological involvement"). Stated properly, inferences carry qualifying language such as, "I think," "It seems to me," or "I feel that . . ." Such language announces the speaker's awareness that the statement is about what the speaker has inferred from the descriptive data and is not a verifiable fact.

It is true that the more descriptive data one has on which to base his or her inference and the more closely related the data are to the inference drawn, the more probable the inference is and the less likely it is to activate another person's defensiveness. For example, the statement, "Jean passed me in the hall this morning and didn't speak; I know she's mad at me" is an inference that has a low probability of being accurate because it is based on only one piece of data, and that one is not necessarily related to anger. The statement, "Jean came into my office frowning, pounded her fist on my desk, and screamed at me, 'I can't believe you could do this to me!' I think she was really angry with me." This also is an inference about Jean's internal state. However, it is an inference that would hardly promote disagreement because it contains more descriptive data which people are likely to agree *are* highly related to anger.

Judgments state the speaker's approval or disapproval, his or her valuing or nonvaluing. Professional judgments usually are based on an estimate of consequences derived from description and inference. As such, judgments need to carry the qualifying language used for inferences (e.g., "I think your child needs . . .," "I feel you've made a wise decision," etc.).

When professionals accurately state their inferences and judgments, it tends to prevent two common errors that can cause parents to become defensive. First, the speaker is less likely to give the impression of dogmatic certainty, which usually makes the other person want to plant his or her intellectual and psychological feet and resist. Second, more accurate statements tend to prevent misuse of what Gordon (1975) called "I statements" and "You statements." "You" statements should be limited to what the other person said or did, whereas "I" statements refer to the speaker's behavior, inferences, and judgments.

The following examples contrast appropriate and inappropriate statements of inference and judgment based on the same descriptive data. The following inferences and judgments are drawn from this descriptive data: "Tom has missed three of his last five treatment sessions."

1. *Inference that seems appropriate*:
    "I think you must be having some trouble with Tom's treatment schedule."

2. *Inference that seems inappropriate:*
   "You don't really care whether or not Tom has this treatment, do you?"

3. *Judgment that seems appropriate:*
   "I really don't like to schedule these appointments and then have Tom miss so many of them."

4. *Judgment that seems inappropriate:*
   "You are very inconsiderate of my time to accept this schedule and then just not show up."

Although these examples may seem extreme, they are similar to many that we have heard professionals use, and we think there is hardly anyone who would not feel attacked with the statements noted as inappropriate. Professionals must use caution in making statements of inference and judgment, and use "I" and "you" appropriately, because people, including parents, justifiably become defensive in the face of dogmatism and misuse of "I" and "you."

Looking for and Stating Areas of Agreement

Conflict can arise when people have different points of view, experiences, motivations, or backgrounds. In the face of conflict, finding and stating areas on which people can agree can often cool the emotional temperatures of each person. Working from areas of agreement makes possible a more successful negotiation and resolution of the conflict.

A teacher, Joan, reported using this principle of finding areas of agreement with a successful outcome. She scheduled a conference with the father of a young boy, Jim, in her preschool class. The teacher wanted to refer Jim for psychological testing. When she told Jim's father of her wish to make this referral, the father became irate, stating, "My son is *not* crazy!" After the teacher said she couldn't agree more that Jim was not crazy, the discussion of her purposes could proceed. She described some of Jim's behaviors, such as lack of consistent attention to a task, and asked the father whether he had noticed these behaviors at home. The father said, "Oh, yes, if you mean like he doesn't pay attention? Usually when I tell him to bring me his shoes so I can put them on him, he goes to his room but forgets to bring back the shoes." He and the teacher then discussed other behaviors they both had observed. Then the teacher said, "We both want ways of finding how best to help Jim, right?" Jim's father agreed, and the teacher repeated her thought that psychological testing might help them help Jim. The father seemed to calm down, and he and the teacher were able to discuss consequences of various alternatives. The father said he would think about psychological testing and later called the teacher to say he agreed with her recommendation.

It is not always easy for professionals to remember the principle of negotiation in situations of conflict, especially when they are feeling defensive. However, if professionals can manage their own defensiveness sufficiently to enter into negotiation, it can often reduce parents' defensiveness and lead to constructive outcomes. Thus negotiation is a skill worth practicing.

Distinguishing Between Intent and Consequence

In verbal interaction, a speaker's well-intentioned statement often is interpreted negatively by the listener. Such dissonance between speaker's intent and the consequence to a listener accounts for much human conflict.

People generally tend to assume that the meaning another person's message has for them is true to the meaning the speaker intends to convey. This assumption happens most often when the listener, from his or her defensiveness, expects negative judgment.

Jumping to such conclusions happens in various kinds of verbal interaction and, unfortunately, blocks further constructive communication. An example occurred recently when a mother reported to one professional that another professional had made a change in her child's treatment plan. In her surprise about the change, the professional receiving the report said, "If he made a change like that, something must have happened since I talked to him last week." The mother blurted out, "I am *not* a liar!" It had never occurred to the professional that the way she stated her surprise, with "*If* he made . . .," would have implied she thought the mother was lying. It took some explanation on the part of the professional to come to an understanding that the professional's intent in the message was different from the consequence of it to the mother. The situation did get clarified when the professional could say, "I'm sorry. I should not have said, 'if.' It would have been better for me to say, 'I'm surprised that he changed his plans since I talked with him, but I'm sure he had reasons I don't yet know.'"

There are many less explosive situations in which it is helpful to assume that the speaker's intent may *not* be what was communicated. Use of questions, such as "Are you saying . . .?" or statements, such as "Tell me how you've understood what I was saying," can express awareness of the principle of separating intent and consequence. This principle should be part of professionals' thinking in giving and responding to messages because it can help to avoid or reduce conflict.

Expressing Compassion Rather than Distant Neutrality

Those who train professionals often warn them against becoming emotionally involved with clients. Certainly there are many ways in which professionals should not get emotionally involved with clients. However, compassion is a special kind of emotional involvement which we encourage professionals to enter into.

Compassion is not the same as sympathy in which one person feels the same emotion as another; that is, if one person expresses anger the other person gets his or her own anger stirred up. Rather, compassion means being comfortable enough with one's own emotions to be able to participate in the *meaning* another person's emotions have for him or her, without getting one's own similar feelings all mixed up in the interaction. As such, compassion is perhaps the most mature of all emotions.

One does not need to have had the same experiences as another person to feel compassion for that person. There is such a vast universe of experiences that no one can duplicate those of another person. However, the range of emotions is much narrower than that of experience. Furthermore, although each person will feel his or her own variation of an emotion, all persons can experience all the emotions. For example, one professional asked, "How can I talk with that mother? I don't have a child, much less one who is overactive. How can I help?" This professional was asked in return whether she had ever felt disappointed, frustrated, hopeful, or out of control. When the professional answered, "Oh, yes, of course!" she was reminded that knowing about these emotions could help her understand what the mother could have felt and was the important connecting point between them.

Parents of children with disabilities certainly need compassion from professionals. In contrast, perceptions of a professional as cold or distantly neutral tend to arouse parents' defensiveness and thus decrease their openness and trust of that professional. Understandably, professionals, who deal so regularly with emotionally difficult situations, can develop a distance to protect themselves. However, many parents have reported experiences with professionals who have been so distant as to seem coldly uncaring. For example, one mother said, "I was told about my daughter's cleft palate in a manner that might have been used to say, 'It's raining today.' I didn't say much then because I really wanted to hit that man and scream, 'It's my *baby* you're talking about!'"

Just as such distance is communicated in both verbal and nonverbal ways, so also is compassion. Certainly the mother in the above example did not feel understood by that professional. Conversely, many parents have spoken of valuing professionals for their skill in communicating compassion without interfering with the business that must be transacted. Of course, compassion must be genuine if it is to be helpful.

Compassionate behavior can serve an important function in helping a parent to see a professional as open and direct rather than having a hidden agenda for the parent and, therefore, as untrustworthy. Some people also make it easier than others for professionals to feel and express compassion. However, professionals can work to feel more compassion for parents, and it is a worthy project to work on because of the many benefits compassion can provide.

Promoting a Sense of Equality Rather than Superiority

Of course, people are never equal in all ways; they differ in training, socioeconomic status, or almost any other variable, because each person is unique. However, in any given situation people *can* feel a sense of equality in their particular roles, in their claim to be acknowledged as a person of worth, and in their claim to justice as a participant in a human interaction. Such a sense of equality is essential if parents are to collaborate most effectively with professionals. As they enter an interaction with a professional, many parents feel vulnerable in confronting the specialist. Some parents have reported that they felt "dumb" until a professional made them feel they had something important to contribute.

Professionals can convey a sense of superiority without intending to do so, or they can convey superiority to try to control a situation. This is especially true when the professional is feeling insecure or threatened by the parent and needs to use superiority in training to cope with the insecurity. Insecure professionals have been known to make such comments as, "It will probably be hard for you to understand my report, but I assure you I've had 10 years of experience in this field so I do know about children like yours," or to load their comments with the jargon of their specialty. There are many other ways professionals can subtly "put down" parents while trying, consciously or not, to establish their own capabilities and thus to control a situation in which they fear loss of control.

One situation in which it is very tempting for professionals to try to "pull out all the stops" to establish their superiority occurs when a parent refuses a recommendation the professional thinks is important. No parent knowingly makes poor decisions for his or her child. Sometimes when a parent refuses to follow a recommendation it is because he or she does not have the information needed to make a better decision. Based on the facts the parent has been given, his or her refusal of a recommendation may be understandable. It is the professional's job to make sure the parent has all the information needed to make an informed decision.

In any case, professionals must accept the fact that parents have the final legal right to make decisions concerning their children. When professionals deeply accept this truth, they can handle these situations gracefully. This does not mean that the professional should not forcefully make a case for his or her recommendation. It does mean that the case should be made in an atmosphere in which the parent has an equal right to make his or her own decision. Professionals who hold an attitude of equality with parents inevitably will create such an atmosphere, thus helping to promote parents' openness and trust rather than defensiveness. It is in this atmosphere that the most productive discussion and decision making takes place.

Who Helps the Helper?

To this point the primary thrust of this book has been to help professionals understand and deal effectively with parents of young children with disabilities. However, we recognize that those who choose these professions also carry their own load of cares. Professionals, too, need help and support as they encounter highly stressful situations.

Often colleagues can be a source of such support, and we urge professionals both to request and give each other such help. The functions that professionals serve for parents (discussed in the Introduction to this book) can be served by colleagues for each other. In the case of one professional helping another professional, the functions emphasized probably will be the last three (i.e., receiving information; helping the person to clarify his or her emotions, attitudes, and behaviors; and assisting in changing behaviors and attitudes that the person needs or wants to change). Such help should be freely requested, freely given, and freely received.

Recognizing that there are many work settings in which professionals do not have colleagues close by, we encourage professionals to take the time to hunt up colleagues with whom they can talk openly and constructively at staff meetings, conventions, inservice meetings, and so on.

Moursund (1990) discussed dilemmas faced by psychotherapists as they worked to help their clients. Moursund emphasized the need for everyone in the helping professions to be committed to continued understanding of themselves. She, too, encouraged professionals in all areas to look for colleagues with whom to talk when confronting dilemmas.

The principles of constructive communication discussed in this chapter represent a direction professionals can take, not only with parents but also with each other. Furthermore, these principles represent a direction to which we commit ourselves rather than a place where we arrive.

We will continue to make mistakes in our work with parents of children with disabilities. Let us have the courage and flexibility to try to learn from our own mistakes and to be compassionate and constructive in our dealings with our colleagues' blunders. Let us also learn not to overlook or downplay our successes, but to rejoice in them. To the extent that we can do these things, we can continue to find pleasure in making life a little better for parents of children with disabilities and for each other.

Suggested Readings

Bailey, D. (1987). Collaborative goal-setting with families: Resolving differences in values and goals for services. *Topics in Early Childhood Education, 7,* 59-71.

Patton, B., & Giffin, K. (1981). *Interpersonal communication: Basic text and readings.* New York: Harper & Row.

BIBLIOGRAPHY

Andrews, J., & Andrews, M. (Eds.) (1986). A family-based systematic model for speech-language services. *Seminars in Speech and Language, 7,* 359–365.

Bailey, D. (1987). Collaborative goal-setting with families: Resolving differences in values and priorities for services. *Topics in Early Childhood Special Education, 7,* 59–71.

Bailey, D., & Simeonsson, R. (1988). *Family assessment in early intervention.* Columbus, OH: Merrill.

Bailey, D., McWilliam, P., & Simeonsson, R. (1991). *Implementing family-centered services in early intervention: A team-based model for change.* Chapel Hill: Carolina Institute for Research on Infant Personnel Preparation, University of North Carolina.

Bates, M., & Johnson, C. (1972). *Group leadership: A manual for group counseling leaders.* Denver, CO: Love.

Benjamin, A. (1974). *The helping interview.* Boston: Houghton-Mifflin.

Brazelton, T. (1989). *To listen to a child.* New York: Addison Wesley.

Brinckerhoff, J., & Vincent, L. (1987). Increasing parental decision-making at the individualized program meeting. *Journal of the Division of Early Childhood, 11,* 46–58.

Bitter, G. (1978). *Parents in action.* Washington, DC: The Alexander Graham Bell Association for the Deaf.

Brutten, M., Richardson, S., & Mangel, C. (1973). *Something's wrong with my child.* New York: Harcourt Brace Jovanovich.

Buscaglia, L. (1975). *The disabled and their parents: A counseling challenge.* Thorofare, NJ: Charles B. Slack

Crais, E. (1991). Moving from "parent involvement" to family centered services. *American Journal of Speech-Language Pathology, 1,* 5–8.

Crutcher, D. (1991). Family support in the home: Home visiting and public law 99–457, a parent's perspective. *American Psychologist, 46*(2), 138–140.

Duncan, L. (1990). Helping friends who grieve. *Woman's Day*, Oct. 2. New York: Hachette Publications.

Faber, A., & Mazlish, E. (1980). *How to talk so kids will listen and listen so kids will talk*. New York: Avon.

Gallagher, J. (1989). A new policy initiative: Infants and toddlers with handicapping conditions. *American Psychologist, 44*(2), 387–391.

Gendlin, E. (1981). *Focusing* (pp. 118–144). New York: Bantam.

Gordon, S. (1988). *When living hurts*. New York: Dell.

Gordon, T. (1975). *P.E.T.: Parent effectiveness training*. New York: The New American Library.

Grater, H., & Claxton, D. (1976). Counselor's empathy level and client topic changes. *Journal of Counseling Psychology, 23*(4), 407–408.

Guardini, R. (1990). *Back to the family*. New York: Random House.

Harry, B. (1992). *Cultural diversity, families, and the special education system: Communication and empowerment*. New York: Teachers College Press.

Hartup, W. (1989). Social relationships and their developmental significance. *American Psychologist, 44*(2), 120–133.

Heisler, V. (1972). *A handicapped child in the family: A guide for parents*. New York: Grune & Stratton.

Hickey, M. (1992). Living with a "wild child." *Working Mother, 15*(5), 62–66.

Horney, K. (1965). *The neurotic personality of our time*. New York: W. W. Norton.

Hutchins, V., & McPherson, M. (1991). National agenda for children with special health needs: Social policy for the 90's through the 21st century. *American Psychologist, 46*, 141–143.

Irby, R. (1985, August). *Educating the handicapped infant*. Paper presented at the International Congress on Education of the Deaf, Manchester, England.

Kjerland, L, & Kovach, J. (1990). Family-staff collaboration for tailored infant assessment. In E. Gibbs & D. Tetti (Eds.), *Interdisciplinary assessment of infants: A guide for early intervention professionals.* Baltimore: Brookes.

Karen, R. (1992). Shame. *The Atlantic, 269*(2), 40–70.

Kushner, H. (1981). *When bad things happen to good people.* New York: Avon.

Landeman, S., & Ramey, C. (1989). Developmental psychology and mental retardation. *American Psychologist, 44*(2), 409–415.

Lang, D. (1990). *Family harmony: Coping with your "challenging" relatives.* New York: Prentice-Hall.

Lavin, P. (1989). *Parenting the overactive child: Alternatives to drug therapy.* New York: Madison.

Lewis, M. (1992). *Shame: The exposed self.* New York: The Free Press.

Luterman, D. (1970). *Counseling parents of hearing-impaired children.* Boston: Little, Brown.

Luterman, D. (1991). *Counseling the communicatively disordered and their families.* Austin, TX: PRO-ED.

Marshall, G., & Herbert, M. (1981). Recorded telephone messages: A way to link teacher and parents. An evaluation report prepared for CEMREL, Washington, DC.

Martin, A. (1977). Post-diagnostic parent counseling by a speech pathologist and a social worker. *Asha, 19*(2), 67–68.

Masterson, J., Swirbul, T., & Noble, D. (1990). Computer generated information packets for parents. *Language, Speech, and Hearing Services in Schools, 21,* 114–115.

McDonald, E. (1962). *Understand those feelings.* Pittsburgh, PA: Stanwix.

Minner, S., & Prater, G. (1987). Parental use of telephone answering equipment to assist handicapped children: Techniques. *A Journal for Remedial Education and Counseling, 3,* 51–56.

Moller, K., Starr, C., & Johnson, S (1990). *A parent's guide to cleft lip and palate.* Minneapolis: University of Minnesota.

Moursund, J. (1990). *The process of counseling and therapy* (2nd ed.). Englewood Cliffs, NJ: Prentice-Hall.

Naiman, D., & Schein, J. (1978). *For parents of deaf children.* Silver Spring, MD: National Association for the Deaf.

Patton, B., & Giffin, K. (1981). *Interpersonal communication in action: Basic text and readings.* New York: Harper & Row.

Roberts, R., Wasik, B., Casto, C., & Ramey, C. (1991). Family support in the home: Programs, policy, and social change. *American Psychologist, 46,* 131–137.

Rogers, C. (1977). The characteristics of a helping relationship. In D. Avila, A. Combs, & W. Purkey (Eds.). *The helping relationship.* New York: Houghton-Mifflin.

Rogow, S. (1988). *Helping the visually impaired child with developmental problems: Effective practice in home, school, and community.* New York: Teachers College Press.

Rollin, W. (1987). *The psychology of communication disorders in individuals and their families.* Englewood Cliffs, NJ: Prentice-Hall. (Chapters 7 & 9)

Samalin, N. (1991). *Love and anger: The parental dilemma.* New York: Viking.

Schubel, R., & Erickson, J. (1992). Model programs for increasing parent involvement through telephone technology. *Language, Speech, and Hearing Services in Schools, 23*(4), 125–129.

Shelton, T., Jeppson, E., & Johnson, B. (1989). *Family centered care for children with special health care needs.* Washington, DC: Association for the Care of Children's Health.

Shontz, F. (1965). Reaction to crisis. *The Volta Review, 67,* 364–370.

Simmons-Martin, A. (1976). A demonstration home approach with hearing impaired children. In E. Webster

(Ed.), *Professional approaches with parents of handi-capped children*. Springfield, IL: Charles C. Thomas.

Smith, P. (1984). *You are not alone: For parents when they learn that their child has a handicap*. Washington, DC: National Information Center for Children and Youth.

Stewart, J. (1974). *Counseling parents of exceptional children*. New York: MSS Publishing.

Stone, J., & Olswang, L. (1989, June-July). The hidden challenge in counseling. *Asha, 31*, 27–31.

Strahan, C., & Zytowski, D. (1976). Impact of visual, vocal, and lexical cues on judgments of counselor qual-ities. *Journal of Counseling Psychology, 23*(4), 387–393.

Tavris, C. (1982). *Anger: The misunderstood emotion*. New York: Simon & Schuster.

Thal, D., Bates, E., & Bellugi, U. (1989). Language and cognition in two children with Williams syndrome. *Journal of Speech & Hearing Research, 32*, 489–500.

Todd, M., & Gottlieb, M. (1976). Interdisciplinary coun-seling in a medical setting. In E. Webster (Ed.), *Profes-sional approaches with parents of handicapped children*. Springfield, IL: Charles C. Thomas.

Turnbull, K., & Hughes, D. (1990). *Families, profession-als, and exceptionality*. Columbus, OH: Merrill.

Webster, E. (1977). *Counseling with parents of handi-capped children: Guidelines for improving communica-tion*. New York: Grune & Stratton.

Webster, E. (1989). How well does your child hear? *Parent and Preschooler*. New York: Preschool Publications, Inc.

Webster, E. (1989). Parent counseling: One more chal-lenge. *The Clinical Connection, 3*(4), 1–3.

Wilcox, M. (1984). Developmental language disorders: Preschoolers. In A. Holland (Ed.), *Language disorders in children*. San Diego, CA: College-Hill Press.

Wilcox, M. (in press). Enhancing initial communication skills in young children with developmental disabilities through partner programming. *Seminars in Speech and Hearing*.

Wing, L. (1972). *Autistic children: A guide for parents.* New York: Brunner/Mazel.

Wyatt, G. (1976). Parents and siblings as co-therapists. In E. Webster (Ed.), *Professional approaches with parents of handicapped children.* Springfield, IL: Charles C. Thomas.

INDEX